4/76

W9-ABV-515

PIRATES

David Mitchell

PIRATES

with 86 illustrations, 15 in colour, and 4 maps

THAMES AND HUDSON
LONDON

For Jason and Christopher

This book is sold subject to the condition that it shall not, by way of trade or otherwise, be lent, re-sold, hired out or otherwise circulated, without the publisher's prior consent, in any form of binding or cover other than that in which it is published, and without a similar condition including these words being imposed on a subsequent purchaser.

© 1976 Thames and Hudson Ltd, London

All rights reserved. No part of this publication may be reproduced or transmitted in any form or by any means, electronic or mechanical, including photocopy, recording or any information storage and retrieval system, without permission in writing from the publisher.

Filmset by Keyspools Limited, Golborne, Lancashire

Printed by FEP International Ltd, Singapore

Contents

Acknowledgments

I am indebted to the staffs of the London Library, the Library of the National Maritime Museum, the Vaughan Williams Memorial Library, and Canning House Library (Belgrave Square), also to Mr and Mrs Roger Low and Mrs Julia Trowbridge, for their kindness and patience.

David Mitchell
June 1975

Chapter One **Soundings**

'Wading towards him hip deep through the waters . . . was a posse of pirates. They were tall as trees, their great brows beetling over their sunken eyes like shelves of overhanging rocks. In their ears were hoops of red gold, and in their mouths scythe-edged cutlasses a-drip. . . . Still they came on, until there was only room enough for the smouldering head of the central buccaneer, a great salt-water lord, every inch of whose face was scabbed and scarred like a boy's knee, whose teeth were carved into the shape of skulls, whose throat was circled by the tattooing of a scaled snake . . .'

Thus, in *Gormenghast*, Mervyn Peake describes a daydream of Titus, 77th Earl of Groan. Generations of children – and adults – have shared and relished a romantic vision of this kind. Its literary origins can be traced to a few pirate ballads of the sixteenth and seventeenth centuries, and to certain passages in *A General History of the Robberies and Murders of the Most Notorious Pirates* by Captain Charles Johnson (alias Daniel Defoe), that prime and often unacknowledged source of so many subsequent writings on the subject, with its marvellous glimpses of the pirate as hell-raising outcast.

Of William Lewis, a contemporary of Blackbeard, Defoe tells that while pursuing a merchantman in the Gulf of Guinea 'an accident happened that made his men believe he dealt with the Devil; for a shot carried away his fore and main-top mast, and Lewis, running up the shrouds to the main-top, tore off a handful of hair, and throwing it to the winds, used this expression, *Good Devil, take this till I come.* And it was observed that he came afterwards faster up with the chase than before.' Charles Bellamy, another early eighteenth-century pirate, is shown defying the elements during a storm terrific enough 'to strike a dread of the Supreme Being, who commands the sea and the winds, in every heart. But among these wretches the effect was very different, for they endeavoured by their blasphemies, oaths and horrid imprecations to drown the uproar. . . . Bellamy swore he was sorry he could not run out his guns to return the salute, meaning the thunder, but he fancied the Gods had got drunk over their tipple and were gone together by the ears.'

The professional Romantics of the nineteenth century, notably Lord Byron in his poem 'The Corsair' (1814) and Sir Walter Scott in his novel *The Pirate* (1822), worked up the theme. Byron was fantasizing from the activities of petty Greek and Turkish corsairs just before the Greek war of independence, but for many years his largely autobiographical version of the despotic Pirate Chief as the victim – and implacable enemy – of society was the popularly accepted one:

7

That man of loneliness and mystery,
Scarce seen to smile and seldom heard to sigh,
Whose name appals the fiercest of his crew
And tints each swarthy cheek with sallow hue,
Still sways their souls with that commanding art
That dazzles, leads, yet chills the vulgar heart . . .
What should it be that thus their faith can bind?
The power of Thought, the magic of the Mind!
Link'd with success, assumed and kept with skill,
That moulds another's weakness to its will,
Wields with their hands, but still to these unknown,
Makes even their mightiest deeds appear his own . . .
Such hath it been, shall be, beneath the sun,
The many still must labour for the one!
'Tis Nature's doom, but let the wretch who toils
Accuse not, hate not, him who wears the spoils.
Oh! If he knew the weight of splendid chains,
How light the balance of his humbler pains! .

Following Byron and Scott, historians and novelists tended to concentrate on the exotic and the picturesque, usually combining this with a stiff moral sermon. Charles Ellms, a Boston stationer, summed up the romantic-moralistic approach in the preface to his best-selling compilation, *The Pirates' Own Book* (1837). 'In the mind of the mariner', he wrote, 'there is a superstitious horror connected with the name of Pirate; and there are few subjects that interest and excite the curiosity of mankind more than the desperate exploits, foul doings, and diabolical careers of these monsters in human form. . . . The pirate is truly fond of women and wine; and when not engaged in robbery keeps maddened with intoxicating liquors and passes his time in debauchery amongst the lofty forests of palms and spicy groves of the Torrid Zone. He has fruits delicious to the taste, and as his companions the unsophisticated daughters of Africa and the Indies.' In conclusion, Ellms was careful to remind readers that 'every man, civilized or savage, has interwoven in his constitution a moral sense which secretly condemns him when he has committed an atrocious crime, even when placed in situations which raise him above the fear of human punishment.'

In the 1850s the Christian Socialist Charles Kingsley idealized the workers' co-operative (or 'alternative society') aspect of piracy in his poem 'The Last Buccaneer':

Captain William Lewis offers a handful of his hair to the Devil: an illustration from The Pirates' Own Book *(1837) typifying the Romantic conception of the pirate as daemonic outcast.*

Oh England is a pleasant place for them that's rich and high,
But England is a cruel place for such poor folk as I;
And such a port for mariners I ne'er shall see again
As the pleasant Isle of Avès beside the Spanish Main.

There were forty craft in Avès that were both swift and stout,
All furnish'd well with small arms and cannons round about;
And a thousand men in Avès made laws so fair and free,
To choose their valiant captains and obey them loyally. . . .

And in *Westward Ho!*, a book animated by an aggressive patriotism
and a still more aggressive Protestantism (he could not think of a
Roman Catholic except as a kind of villain), Kingsley consolidated
the myth of the Elizabethan sea-dogs as noble crusaders for the
Reformed Faith to whom plunder was a religious and patriotic duty.

In *Treasure Island* (1883) Stevenson does not indulge in much
moralizing, but he does at times play up the Romance of Piracy.
There is Long John Silver's fabulous parrot ('Maybe two hundred
years old, and if anybody's seen more wickedness it must be the devil
himself'), and the awesome Captain Flint, beside whom 'Blackbeard
was a child'. The real fallacy, however, is in the title. Silver
emphasizes that pirates 'lives rough and risks swinging – but when a
cruise is done, why it's hundreds of pounds instead of hundreds of
farthings in their pockets, though the most goes for rum and a good
fling and to sea again in their shirts': yet the book revolves round the
assumption (completely exploded by Ellms) that pirates had the time
or the inclination to be provident and that their booty was always in
the form of gold and finger-trickling treasure.

In *The Fortunes of Captain Blood* (1936), a highly entertaining
myth-spinner, Rafael Sabatini, though showing a firm grasp of some
of the realities of buccaneering, constructed a Byronic version of the
pirate captain as a victim of social injustice (Blood had been
transported to the West Indies for his part in Monmouth's Rebellion)
wielding absolute authority over his crew: and John Masefield,
though he wrote authoritatively about pirates, is probably best
remembered for two verses from his poem 'Cargoes' epitomizing
the lovely loot which the pirates of romantic legend – enviably free
spirits operating in a political and economic vacuum – are forever
getting their hands on:

Quinquireme of Nineveh from distant Ophir,
Rowing home to haven in sunny Palestine,
With a cargo of ivory,
And apes and peacocks,
Sandalwood, cedarwood, and sweet white wine.

Stately Spanish galleon, coming from the Isthmus,
Dipping through the Tropics by the palm-green shores,
With a cargo of diamonds,
Emeralds, amethysts,
Topazes and cinnamon and gold moidores.

The seductive simplicity of legends seems doomed to erosion by
historical research. Like land-brigandage, sea-robbery no doubt

began when commerce started to make some people richer in possessions than others. It has been conjectured that the first water-borne snatch probably took place 'in the far, dim ages, when some naked savage, paddling himself across a tropical river, met with another adventurer on a better tree-trunk or carrying a bigger bunch of bananas'. As commerce got more complex and sophisticated, so did piracy. In due course, pirate gangs banded together under acknowledged leaders and piracy became big business. There were Treasure Islands, though not in Stevenson's sense – in ancient Crete, for example, organized piracy formed the economic basis of a flourishing civilization. But 'pure' pirates – sea-going outlaws playing a lone hand against all comers 'without political purpose or official authority' (as the 1971 edition of the *Encyclopaedia Britannica* puts it) – were increasingly rare.

The word 'pirate' derives from the Greek *peiran*, meaning to attempt or attack, and the Laws of Solon (*c.* 594 BC) refer to authorized associations of pirates. There was no lack of official employment for them. The authorities of the city states could not afford to fit out regular fleets and therefore relied on pirates to fight naval wars on commission (the Athenian tax-gathering squadrons were largely manned by professional freebooters who knew every inlet, headland and shallow and were used to extorting tribute). Merchants whose goods had been stolen were empowered to take reprisals to the estimated value of their missing cargoes. Often they did not wait for a licence or commission – which had to be paid for – and many merchant vessels habitually combined trade with plunder as the only really effective insurance policy. The pattern that was to become so familiar had already taken shape and in fact, if not in name, the privateering system was well established.

Employers' and employees' shares in the prospective loot would be fixed before the start of a voyage, but there were plenty of opportunities for cheating. Crews were liable to 'exceed their commissions' (that is, not to confine their attentions to the enemy or enemies stipulated in their contracts). Injured parties could be assured that the commissioners were not responsible for these 'mistakes' and courts set up to afford a time- and money-consuming show of justice. But double-dealing did not end there. Employers could never be sure that some of the booty would not be concealed or disposed of before returning to base, thus reducing their dividend.

In England the first letters of marque, or reprisal, were issued in the thirteenth century, but for four hundred years after that the boundaries between legitimate trade, reprisal, and outright piracy were blurred, often to the point of invisibility. The same person might well be trader, fisherman, pirate and naval employee by turns. During the Middle Ages open warfare between rival corsair centres was common. St Malo was at loggerheads with Boulogne. The Cinque Ports of Sussex and Kent – Hastings, Romney, Hythe, Dover and Sandwich – flagrantly abused the privileges they were granted in return for furnishing a quota of ships for the royal service, and their indiscriminate pillaging was challenged, and imitated, by the men of Yarmouth, Plymouth and Fowey.

In the wake of the Iberian pioneers, 'adventuring' (as the have-nots liked to call their murderous determination to share the loot of the New World) went oceanic. French, Dutch and English veterans of the interminable scrimmages in home waters extended their operations, and for the next two centuries they and their Carib-beanized successors, the buccaneers, seldom lacked a commission of sorts. From 1494, when the Treaty of Tordesillas, blessed by a Spanish Pope, divided the New World between Spain and Portugal, it was axiomatic that there was 'no peace beyond the Line' – drawn west of the Azores and north of the Tropic of Cancer. After the Reformation the Catholic-Protestant split added religious sanction to commercial frustration. Any sea-going cut-throat could call himself a crusader, though for nearly two centuries – until the back of Spanish resistance had been broken – French Catholic pirates made common cause with *corsarios luteranos*. Similarly, in the Mediter-ranean after the battle of Lepanto (1571), the Muslim-Christian confrontation continued in the form of a desultory war of corsair 'crusaders' operating from the Barbary coast of North Africa, Malta (the Knights of St John) and Leghorn (the Knights of St Stephen).

Privateering seemed an ideal arrangement to semi-feudal prince-lings and to Tudor and Stuart monarchs chronically short of cash. It cost nothing and was actually a source of revenue in the form of royal and admiralty dues. Laws against piracy remained dead letters. There was no navy to enforce them, since for all practical purposes the pirates were the navy. It was plausibly argued that 'roving' kept them in practice for the next war or privateering cruise, and until at least the end of the sixteenth century the gentry of the south coast of England, the Welsh seaboard, and the east coast of Ireland controlled and invested in piratical operations and were well able to protect their employees. Though a few obscure pirates might be hanged from time to time, not a single captain of note or connections suffered more than a petty fine. If every person directly or indirectly involved in piracy had suffered the penalty demanded by the law, the south coast of England would have been virtually depopulated and the Spanish Armada would have met with little opposition.

To hear the slippery subjects of one's study tell it, none of them was really a pirate at all: at worst they were self-appointed privateers combining patriotic initiative with personal advantage, and the almost infinite scope of some commissions helped to encourage this attitude. King James I (known as the Peacemaker) made some attempt to restrain attacks on Spanish shipping, but commissioned piratical expeditions to the Red Sea and the Persian Gulf and took his share of the plunder. In 1630 Charles I licensed Captain Quail of the *Seahorse* to 'make purchase [i.e. plunder] in the Red Sea, as well as anywhere else, of any he can meet with that are not friends or allies of

After capturing Blackbeard in November 1718, Lt. Maynard of HMS Pearl had him decapitated and fixed the head to the bowsprit as a trophy.

His Majesty'. The profit from the cruise of the *Seahorse* was estimated at around £75,000.*

In 1634 two more ships were royally commissioned 'to range the seas all over and to make prize of all such treasure, merchandise, goods and other commodities which they shall be able to take of infidels or of any other prince, potentate, or state not in league or amity with us beyond the line equinoctial'. The first prize taken was a Mogul vessel with a safe-conduct issued by the East India Company at Bombay. According to the Company's report, the captain and crew were persuaded to tell where their treasure was hidden by 'binding their fingers together with wire and putting lighted matches between them until they were burnt to the bone'. Since the Company was likely to suffer reprisals ashore after such incidents, it complained

* This and other estimates of sixteenth- to eighteenth-century prize-yields should be multiplied by *c.* 25–35 to get an approximate present-day equivalent.

bitterly about the behaviour of 'the King's pirates', though its own 'privateers' had not hesitated to use much worse tortures.

It was not surprising that men caught and condemned as pirates – and contrary to popular belief comparatively few were – shared their alleged betters' sense of racial and religious superiority and pleaded it in extenuation of any kind of excess. Chaplains who attended pirate hangings at Wapping Old Stairs (Execution Dock) in the 1690s reported that some malefactors 'expressed contrition for the horrid barbarities they had committed, though only on the bodies of heathens', while others, though they repented swearing and profaning the Sabbath, did not feel guilty of piracy since 'they had not known but it was lawful to plunder ships and goods belonging to the enemies of Christianity'.

A hanging at Execution Dock, London – a comparatively rare occurrence considering the prevalence of piracy.

Nicholas Hilliard's miniature (1581) of Sir Francis Drake, the super-pirate who became a national hero and Protestant paladin.

Trying to define piracy is like trying to catch an eel or wading into a semantic morass. Euphemisms abound – 'roving', 'being at the seas', 'going on the account' – and confusion is never far away: in the sixteenth century 'man-of-war' was the term for a pirate or privateer, while 'corsair' is generally used as a synonym for 'pirate', sometimes as a synonym for 'privateer'. Philip Gosse, one of the first writers to attempt a comprehensive coverage, complained that it came perilously close to being a maritime history of the world. Samuel Taylor Coleridge, never one to flinch from a portentous generalization, acquitted the Elizabethan corsairs of piracy on the ground that 'no

man is a pirate unless his contemporaries agree to call him so.' This dictum recognizes that there are fashions in morals, but ignores the fact that points of view vary in space as well as time. Spain did not distinguish between privateers and pirates. The ruling was that all trespassers in the forbidden waters were pirates who, if captured, were to be hanged – with their commissions round their necks.

A poster for Gilbert and Sullivan's The Pirates of Penzance, *dating from around 1920 – a popular, picturesque view of piracy which can be traced right back to sixteenth-century ballads.*

One did not need to be a Spaniard to realize that the division between pirates and privateers was paper-thin, since the same men and the same motives were involved on either side of it. The Rev. Cotton Mather, in a sermon preached at Boston in 1704, observed that 'the Privateering Stroke so easily degenerates into the Piratical, and the Privateering Trade is usually carried on with an UnChristian Temper and proves an Inlet into so much Debauchery and Iniquity'. Nor was the distinction between privateering, piracy and regular naval operations very precise. Nelson grumbled that 'the conduct of all privateers is, as far as I have seen, so near piracy that I only wonder any civilized nation can allow them.' But this was sour grapes rather than righteous indignation. The prospect of plunder was an important incentive to enter the royal service, and privateers reduced the chances of a satisfactory fall of what Drake called 'some little comfortable dew from heaven'.

Drake was a hero to Englishmen and a pirate to Spaniards, just as John Paul Jones was a hero to Americans and a pirate to Englishmen. Official attitudes have varied according to circumstances. During the Middle Ages England claimed supremacy in 'the English Seas', but by Elizabeth's time was, in the name of free trade and fair shares, self-righteously contesting the Iberian monopoly of the waters of the New World. After 1815 the possession of a powerful navy (and a 'civilizing mission') enabled Britain to define any attempt at resistance to her imperial whims as piracy (or banditry). There was nothing new in this. Powers with imperial pretensions had always branded their rivals as pirates. The Phoenicians, the Greeks and the Romans all used rhetoric about a civilizing mission. The story goes that when Alexander the Great asked a captured pirate what right he had to infest the seas, the man replied: 'The same right you have to infest the world.' The Roman lawyer Cicero seems to have got in first with the definition of pirates as *hostes humani generis* (enemies of the human race – i.e. of Rome), a formula which proved very useful to Rome's imperial successors. Similar arguments were used by Spain, Portugal, and a tenuously united Arab Front under the leadership of the Ottoman Empire. The imperial ambitions of Venice in the eastern Mediterranean invited, and got, a deadly challenge from the corsairs of both Malta and Barbary, with enthusiastic help from the heavily-armed merchant ships of England and Holland – all of them, in the eyes of the Venetian Senate, nothing but pirates.

In the Far East, the Celestial Empire's efforts to exclude 'barbarian pirates' provoked massive Viking-like raids by Japanese corsair fleets whose crews wore uniforms of red coats and yellow caps and ranged

Antigua in the West Indies: earthly paradise to the promoters of colonization, den of iniquity to nineteenth-century moralists who pictured pirates living 'in debauchery amongst the lofty forests of palms'.

as far south as the Straits of Malacca. Not until the seventeenth century were their depredations checked, and then only by precarious alliances with Portuguese free-traders – who looked just like pirates to those at the wrong end of the cannon.

Definitions could differ in a pirate's own country, but nothing succeeded, or exonerated, like success. When Francis Drake returned to England in 1580 from a voyage round the world in which he combined exploration and market surveys with a veritable orgy of plunder, his fate trembled in the balance for six months. If, like Raleigh some forty years later, he had failed in the treasure hunt, he might well have been executed rather than knighted. But the *Golden Hind*'s treasure take was valued at £600,000, perhaps about £20 million in today's terms. Sheer bulk of loot swayed the verdict – just the consideration by which a pirate company judged its captain.

Attempts to define the status of sea-robbery by the degree of humanity shown in the course of it are not very helpful. Apologists have defended Drake's marauds by explaining that he was a 'great man', patriotic, God-fearing, and merciful by the standards of his time. This could make him an unusual type of pirate – if one accepts the 'decks-awash-with-gore' image. But the evidence is that, contrary to legend, many pirates did not kill, or even fight, unless they were forced to. The avoidance of mortality, and of damage to a valuable cargo in a ship which he might want to take over, was a very important part of an efficient pirate's technique.

The most sensible conclusion seems to be that though some commissions were more justifiable than others, pirates and privateers had the same motive – plunder – and that in either category they worked on a 'no-prey-no-pay' basis. The scope of piracy, very narrow on a strictly legalistic interpretation, turns out to be almost embarrassingly wide. One is back, after all, to Gosse's dilemma.

Yet the great age of piracy has fairly precise limits. No doubt the Chinese, the Japanese, the Indians and the Malays have their seagoing villains and noble rovers, their Blackbeards and Drakes, but for westerners 'real' piracy emerges from the mists with the Barbary corsairs and the exultantly documented exploits of French and English raiders in the Caribbean towards the middle of the sixteenth century, and vanishes abruptly in the early 1720s.

Within this crucial span there are six main foci: (i) the Elizabethan corsairs; (ii) the early seventeenth-century English and Dutch renegades in Barbary and Morocco, notably John Ward, Simon Danziker and Jan Jansz; (iii) the Turkish and Moorish corsairs of the Barbary ports (Algiers, Tunis and Tripoli), beginning with the brothers Barbarossa; (iv) the buccaneers, with Pierre le Grand, François Lolonois, Henry Morgan, the Sieur de Grammont, Bartholomew Sharp and William Dampier as the leading figures; (v) the years of the Pirate Round (*c.* 1690–1700) between the ports of the North American colonies and the Indian Ocean, with Thomas Tew,

'Long Ben' Avery and William Kidd as the best-known characters; and (vi) the classic age of piracy (c. 1714–24), with operations in the Caribbean, along the coasts of the Carolinas and Virginia, in the Gulf of Guinea, and again in the Indian Ocean. Blackbeard and Bartholomew Roberts, Howell Davis, Edward England and John Taylor are the big names, with a large supporting cast, among them Charles Bellamy, Henry Vane, 'Calico Jack' Rackham, and the so-called female pirates, Mary Read and Anne Bonny. This is the period immortalized by Defoe and Stevenson.

The last three categories are so closely linked as to form a near-continuous sequence. Their pre-eminence in pirate literature and lore is largely due to two chroniclers of genius, Alexander Exquemelin and Daniel Defoe, and two books, *The Buccaneers of America* and the *General History of Pirates*. It is still not certain whether Exquemelin was French or Dutch by birth. What is established is that in 1666 he went to the island of Tortuga, the buccaneers' first base, as an *engagé* (indentured servant) of the French West India Company, joined the buccaneers as a 'barber-surgeon' in 1669, and sailed with them for the next five years, after which he settled in Holland. His account, originally published in 1678 as *De Americaensche Zee-Rovers*, had a runaway success and was translated into most European languages. Each translation catered for nationalistic foibles. The Spanish version pictured Henry Morgan as a monster of depravity and cruelty and the Spaniards as innocent victims. The English and Dutch versions reversed the roles, inviting 'the curious reader' to note how 'God permitted the unrighteousness of the buccaneers to flourish, for the chastisement of the Spaniards'.

Defoe's impressively accurate wealth of information was sometimes larded with pious Nonconformist sentiment. He did not see his pirates as God's unwitting scourges, but lost no chance to use them as illustrations of the 'eternal Truth' that Crime Does Not Pay – in the end. Since he drew heavily on records of the trials of pirates who had been brought to justice, he was able to give the impression that most of them were 'doomed to be cut short by a sudden precipitation into the next world', as befitted such 'lewd and blasphemous fellows'.

Yet on both authors the mask of stern morality, a well-known literary device to flatter and titillate the 'civilized' reader, is always slipping. Exquemelin writes with nostalgia of the comradeship and egalitarianism of the buccaneers ('if they notice he has better food, the men bring the dish from their own mess and exchange it for the captain's'), and contrasts the meanness and brutality of colonial officials to their slaves, black and white (for indentured servants were treated like slaves), with the comparative freedom and generosity of the Brethren of the Coast. The main difference between the taverns and brothels of Tortuga and those of any European port was that the buccaneers had more money to spend and spent it with mad

Frontispiece of the first Dutch edition (1725) of Defoe's General History, *featuring the Jolly Roger and the so-called female pirates, Mary Read and Anne Bonny.*

20

HISTORIE DER ZEE-ROOVERS.

prodigality ('I have seen one of them offer a common strumpet 500 pieces of eight to see her naked').*

With an eye to the values of thrifty bourgeois readers, Defoe dwells on the gluttony of the pirates, forever seeking oblivion in strong liquor and wasting their ill-gotten gains in 'wanton and riotous living'. Yet his prose positively sparkles when he describes such scenes of cornucopian extravagance as that when, flush with Mogul plunder, Captain Taylor's companies salute John Trumpet, a vendor of high-proof arrack, with 'eleven guns each ship', and throw 'ducatoons by the handful for the boatmen to scramble for'; and having gloated over the death of Blackbeard, he allows himself to reflect: 'Here was an end of that courageous brute, who might have passed in the world for a hero had he been employed in a good cause.'

Defoe and Exquemelin may have fathered a few myths, but, having been involved in or very close to their subject, they were firmly anchored in reality. Both made it clear that a pirate captain was no autocrat but an elected leader liable to instant demotion if he had bad luck (not enough loot) or, in the opinion of the company, showed cowardice or bad judgment. Blackbeard's horrific *persona* was calculated to overawe his crew as much as his victims, and Bartholomew Roberts, a man of immense toughness and resource, complained that pirates elected their captains 'only in order to tyrannize over them'. Unable to take the psychological strain, some reverted to the ranks or split off with their cronies to start the game from scratch.

Tactical decisions were taken in open council, and every shareholder had his say. Except in short bursts of action, when the captain had absolute command, the quartermaster was the real focus of authority, listening to grievances, awarding punishments, supervising share-outs. William Snelgrave, captured off the Guinea Coast in 1719, reported that the crews were up in arms when the pirate captains proposed to borrow his best clothes for a shore visit 'among the negro ladies', and insisted that the garments were put into the common chest in care of the quartermaster. Long John Silver boasts that, as quartermaster, he was the only man feared by Captain Flint.

Though forced by prudence to deal in hints rather than outright statements, Defoe left 'even country readers' in no doubt that the pirates could not have functioned without an extensive network of influential receivers and protectors. He also realized that though plunder – Squire Trelawney's 'Gold! What else?' – was their objective, the pursuit of it, like the pursuit of any master passion, included and released a whole constellation of motives and skills; and a century later Captain James Burney, author of *The History of the Buccaneers of America*, praised these 'miscreants notorious for want of humanity' for their pioneer work as explorers in the Pacific. Because of their achievements in charting coasts, currents, and

* Spanish currency was used throughout the West Indies. There were eight *reales* to a dollar (piece of eight), which would now be worth about £2.50–£3 ($6–$7).

prevailing winds, describing the flora and fauna of unknown regions, and chronicling the customs of outlandish tribes, he extended his approval to William Dampier, Lionel Wafer, Basil Ringrose and Bartholomew Sharp. Most people, however, are not greatly concerned with these scientific by-products of piracy, remarkable as they were. The buccaneers' feats of endurance and navigation in search of loot have another significance, one full of appeal to the inhabitants of an overpopulated and over-policed world – the urge and, thanks to imperfect communications, the chance, if one sailed far enough, to find at least a temporary respite from the inexorable advance of Progress.

Pirates possessed no ideological equipment, unless one counts a raw and penetrating cynicism (which in a sense was Marx's starting-point). Spendthrift and makeshift, they offer an opulence of what might be called moral ambiguity. Like such legendary bandits as Jesse James or Billy the Kid, they can be seen as resourceful but doomed opponents of the frontier-closers and wage-slavers – seedy avengers of whom Brecht's down-trodden kitchen maid, Pirate Jenny, dreams that they will come in an eight-sailed ship, storm the city, and ask her who shall be spared.

The capture of significant amounts of treasure was a rarity, Treasure Island a fantasy. The pirate round was full of boredom, relieved by compulsive gambling, vicious quarrels, and wild binges. Homosexuality was common, syphilis rife, and there were probably more casualties in brothels than in battle. In one of his more bizarre exploits, Blackbeard held hostage several prominent citizens of Charleston, South Carolina, until the Governor delivered an expensive consignment of medicines itemized by the pirates' surgeon: almost certainly they were mercurial preparations for the treatment of venereal disease.

Yet when all the qualifications and adulterations have been made, the power of the pirate myth remains. The pirate seas and islands were exotic; the pirate way of life, though more disciplined than is often imagined, did offer a very attractive alternative to the underpaid and over-lashed crews of naval and merchant ships; there were blood-dripping butchers as well as self-interestedly humane operators; pirate captains often worked miracles of impudent and daring improvisation; and there was an element of revenge or social rebellion as well as greed for gold.

Titus's vision has, after all, a certain validity – children, being natural debauchees, understand perfectly the lust to plunder and squander. And who has not known moods when he might have been tempted by Bartholomew Roberts's specious lure – 'in honest service there are commonly low wages and hard labour; in piracy satiety, liberty and power: and who would not balance creditor on this side when all the hazard they run for it is at worst only a sour look or two at choking?'

Chapter Two **Freedoms on the Seas**

Phoenician galleys traversing the Mediterranean with luxury cargoes from the East came to accept pirate attacks as an occupational hazard : detail from a mural in the palace of Sennacherib.

The Persian Gulf is usually taken to be the first venue of piracy on a large scale. Progressing from oars to sails and gradually extending their range, by about 5000 BC the fishermen of the Oman Gulf were transporting the merchandise of India. By the ninth century BC they were trading with Canton and had established trading posts in Java, Sumatra and Siam, not without a good deal of piratical force and fraud. Cargoes of frankincense, spices (including myrrh for embalming), silks, jewels, gold and silver ware, ivory, teak and copper were re-shipped at Omani ports and carried up the Euphrates to Babylon.

The narrow Straits of Hormuz and the 150 miles of what came to be known as the Pirate Coast, reaching from the Qatar Peninsula to the borders of Oman, were ideal for piracy. With its narrow, twisting creeks, sandbanks and jagged coral reefs, this is a barren, forbidding region, scorching hot in summer, in winter whipped by sandstorm and lashed by gales when the *shamaal* howls from the north. Using swift, manoeuvrable, shallow-draughted craft and knowing all the uncharted hazards, pirates were in a position of almost unassailable strength. The Assyrian king Sennacherib led an expedition against them in the seventh century BC. More than three centuries later Alexander the Great's fleet was harried by them. Roman ships were packed with archers to ward off their attacks. The Emperor Trajan led a naval expedition into the Gulf, ravaging the Pirate Coast, and in the fourth century AD Shapur, King of Persia – known as Zulaklaf, or Lord of the Shoulders, because captured pirates had their shoulders pierced and were strung together with ropes to prevent escape – repeated the performance. For two centuries, from about AD 800, the pirates of the Gulf of Oman and the islands of Bahrain fought as privateers in a series of formidable revolts against the authority of the caliphs in Baghdad. While they swept the seas, Bahraini soldiers captured Mecca and removed the sacred black stone from the Kaaba to Hasba, headquarters of the Carmathian sect.

In the Mediterranean, merchants came to accept pirates as an occupational hazard; and towards the end of the Phoenician era, prizes included silver from Spain, amber from the Baltic, and tin from Britain, as well as the merchandise of the East.

In 580 BC, Greek corsairs established a forward base on the Lipari Islands north of Sicily, evolving there a form of communism in which land was held in common and spoils were divided among the entire population. They worked on one of the key principles of democracy, that of organization by law and locality instead of by custom and

kinship, their fundamental unit being the ship's company. As among the Viking raiders and in the pirate communities of the Caribbean and the Indian Ocean, one gets an exhilarating intimation of that epic, revolutionary interval when family and tribal bonds are snapped and everything outside the company of comrades is seen as an object of plunder and contempt.

The Mediterranean corsairs used much the same tactics as their Arab counterparts, confining their activities to daylight and hugging the coasts. Savage reprisals by the Carthaginians and Etruscans – the stoning of Greek pirates, the drowning of captives with the living bound to the dead (a practice that became a routine punishment for murderers in the English navy) – were paid back in the same coin. So constant in this period were raids and counter-raids that settlements were abandoned, islands evacuated, towns and villages moved inland and heavily fortified. The architecture and town-planning of the Mediterranean littoral was to a large extent dictated by the ever-present corsair menace, and still the raiders reached past the coasts to sack, hold to ransom, and take slaves. In his novel *Aethiopica*, Heliodorus of Emesa describes the pursuit of a Phoenician merchant ship by a Cretan corsair. 'When the wind dropped and we had to row, the barque gained on us. Everyone was at the oars and she was a light boat. Our ship was filled with tumult, lamentations and rushing to and fro. . . . When one of the pirates leapt aboard and cut down a few of our people, and the rest jumped after him, the Phoenicians lost courage and falling flat on their faces begged for mercy.'

This design on a Greek vase is said to show captured pirates being keel-hauled. They were also drowned with the living bound to the dead.

The last hundred years of the Roman Republic saw the most remarkable outburst of piracy, in the form of a direct and powerful challenge to imperialist pretensions, the Mediterranean has known. Based on the seaward slopes of the Taurus range at the southern boundary of the central plateau of Asia Minor, Cilician marauders, allied with King Mithridates of Pontus, blockaded and ravaged the Roman Main. Four hundred towns were sacked, Rome brought to the verge of starvation, the temples of the gods looted. In 78 BC the dandified young Julius Caesar (Sulla called him 'the boy in petticoats') was captured in the Aegean and held prisoner for six weeks on the island of Pharmacusa while his friends raised a heavy ransom.

Other Roman captives were handled more roughly, either because they were not so rich or because their captors decided to indulge a taste for whimsical terrorism. As Defoe puts it, 'if any said he was a Roman, they fell on their knees as in a fright at the greatness of his name, begged pardon for what they had done, and imploring his mercy, performed the offices of servants about his person. When they had deceived him into a belief of their being sincere, they hung out the ladder of the ship, and coming with a great show of courtesy, told him he had his liberty, desiring him to walk out of the ship, and this in the middle of the sea. When they observed him in surprise, as was natural, they used to throw him overboard with mighty shouts of laughter; so wanton were they in their cruelty.' This could be the

origin of the legend that 'walking the plank' was a favourite pirate diversion.

The Cilician threat was not broken, and even then not finally, until the mammoth campaign led in 67 BC by Pompey, whose critics claimed that the expense would wreck the economy of the Republic, and that the emergency powers he demanded would lead to a dictatorship. His engine of retribution consisted of 120,000 foot soldiers, four thousand cavalrymen, and 270 ships divided into thirteen commands that swept the Mediterranean from end to end and patrolled the Black Sea. The naval operations, meticulously planned and rapidly executed, ended in a major sea battle off the Cilician coast and were completed in three months instead of the three years Pompey had estimated. The destruction, like the booty, was enormous: four hundred ships were captured and 1,300 destroyed, more than ten thousand pirates killed and twenty thousand taken prisoner. The task of pacification was helped by Pompey's decision to settle the survivors in agricultural colonies, a solution that was attempted, not very successfully, with the buccaneers of the Caribbean about seventeen centuries later. It was a famous victory, one that kept the sea lanes reasonably clear until the Roman Empire began to disintegrate. But it had been a close call. 'Had the Cilicians overthrown Pompey', wrote Defoe, 'it is likely that Rome, which had conquered the world, might have been subdued by a parcel of pirates.'

Such an effective and ruthless operation was not seen again until the British and American navies' police actions of the nineteenth century: and just as the Pax Britannica made possible, and fashionable, a literary idealization of the Corsair, so the Pax Romana allowed writers like Seneca, Quintilian and Heliodorus to exploit the romantic possibilities of piracy in tales of lovers separated and reunited, high-born beauties preserving their virginity amidst fearful perils, and amorous corsair captains (or corsair captains' daughters).

With the decline of the Roman Empire, commerce-raiding also declined. Not much that travelled by water was worth plundering. The next dramatic surge of seaborne plunderers began nearly four centuries later. The Viking raids were essentially amphibious operations. Danes and Norwegians ravaged the coasts of Ireland, England, Scotland, France, Spain, North Africa and Italy. Swedish warriors, called Rus, a Slav version of the Finnish word *ruotsi* (oarsmen), penetrated to the regions around the Black Sea. In Muslim Iberia the Vikings were known as Madjus – heathen wizards. In the churches and monasteries of northern France people prayed, 'From the wrath of the Northmen, Lord, deliver us.'

Scholars have proposed a fourfold classification of Viking ventures as developing from more or less random pirate raids to politically motivated expeditions, colonizing enterprises and commercial expansion; and have suggested overpopulation and famine as possible causes of the Scandinavian breakout.

Motives were no doubt mixed, and one step led to another. The success of the first raids, led by minor chieftains (elected officers as liable to recall as the pirate captains of the eighteenth century), prompted more ambitious campaigns led or financed by hereditary kings. The organization or 'nationalization' of freebooting enterprise was almost an iron law of piracy. This was the way things had gone in the Persian Gulf and the Mediterranean. This was to be the pattern wherever piratical pioneers demonstrated that returns were high and risks low.

The overriding impression is one of traditional, full-blooded piracy – fire, slaughter, rape, loot, orgy, fierce and exultant irresponsibility. The great Viking captains' names – Eric Bloodaxe, Harald Bluetooth, Swein Forkbeard, Björn Ironside – have a wonderful corsair clang. To these raiders from the north, Christian and Muslim ideas of guilt and sin were meaningless: the Viking gods were friends and allies in a bloody fracas leading, if a man had courage and luck, to death in battle and a place in Valhalla, where slain heroes fought and feasted till the end of time.

A Roman war galley of the kind used by Pompey in his anti-piratical campaign of 67 BC.

To the Norwegian and Danish Vikings, refugees from a stark land and a utility culture, 'the West' was an Eldorado as lust-inflaming as the kingdoms of the Incas to the boorish *conquistadores*. The monasteries of Ireland, England and France were treasure-houses stored with gold and silver ornaments, precious stones and gleaming brocades: and they were the first objectives of a sequence of high-hearted rapine. A single shipload vivid with the spoils of Noirmoustier or Lindisfarne was enough to loosen an avalanche of greed and inaugurate two centuries of Viking 'expansion'. One easy scoop beckoned another in a chain-reaction which seemed to offer almost limitless prospects of loot.

Europe seemed paralysed before an enemy so ferocious and mobile. Norsemen would row up the Thames or the Loire, seize horses from farms, race through the countryside burning, killing and looting, and vanish long before their victims could gather to retaliate. Within the space of a decade their red sails appeared at Hamburg and Bordeaux, Lisbon and Cadiz, Seville, Algeciras and Nekar (Morocco). But the Irish, the Franks and the English learned to exploit the rivalry between Danes and Norwegians when joint operations began and spheres of influence overlapped. The single-mindedness of the early companies was complicated by political second thoughts. A kingdom, it began to seem, was worth a Mass; one did not have to plough the seas to reap a profit. Corsair chiefs, attracted by the legend of Charlemagne and fancying themselves as little Holy Roman Emperors, adopted Christianity and began to settle the lands they had been plundering. Yet under the surface the plunderlust remained. Their descendants, the Normans, were the spearhead of the assault on the Muslim infidels, and the First Crusade, though nominally Catholic, displayed much of the character of a neo-Viking foray.

A medieval painted banner showing 'Saint' Vladimir, rugged descendant of the Swedish Viking pirates who founded Novgorod and Kiev.

The great Swedish swashbuckle followed much the same course. Hired in 862 by the Slavs of eastern Europe to collect taxes from refractory tribes and ward off Turkish nomads, the Rus under Rurik (also known as the Varangians) soon controlled the rivers and lakes from the Baltic to the Black Sea. Established in Novgorod and Kiev, they carried on an extensive slave trade, carved out principalities for themselves, and attempted the conquest of Bulgaria. These masterful auxiliaries convoyed cargoes of furs, slaves and honey down the seven cataracts of the lower Dnieper: but for them the Dnieper was above all the highway to Middlegarth (Byzantium), the wealthiest and mightiest of cities. Four times – in 860, 880, 907 and 914 – Varangian fleets threatened the capital of the Eastern Empire and were fought or bought off. The name Rus was soon applied to the passive Slavs as well as to their new masters and became the common designation of the people of Russia.

Early in the tenth century Ibn Fadlan, an envoy from the Caliph of Baghdad, set down his impressions of the *ruotsi* way of life, which seemed to him a barbaric mixture of cut-throat avarice and bestial lust. A fastidious man, he was disgusted by its filth, lack of privacy, incessant drunkenness, and public sexual orgies. He noted the primitive totem-worship of the Rus, who laid offerings of bread, meat, vegetables, milk and liquor before 'a large wooden stake with a human-type face, surrounded by smaller figures, and behind them tall poles in the ground. Each man prostrates himself and recites: "O Lord, I have come from distant parts with so many girls, so many sable furs etc. Please send me a rich merchant who will do business without too much haggling."'

Yet the days of the old gods were numbered. Varangian mercenaries began to enter the imperial bodyguard in Constantinople, and became the most renowned warriors of the Byzantine state. Through them and through commercial travellers, word came back of the splendours of the Greek Orthodox religion. The switch to Christianity was decreed by Vladimir. Seizing Cherson, he threatened to massacre its inhabitants unless he was given a Byzantine princess to wed: and wed he was in 988 to Anne, sister of the Emperors Basil and Constantine. Returning to Kiev, he ordered the public degradation of Slav idols, supervised a huge collective baptism in the waters of the Dnieper, and determined to make the city a second Middlegarth.

In 1169 Kiev, which by then boasted four hundred gaudy churches, was sacked during a civil war between the many descendants of Ruric to decide who was entitled to rule as Grand Prince. The Rus never became landlords, but remained Danegeld-grabbers and slave-dealers, fighters and traders restless by land and water. Their warring principalities were overwhelmed by the hordes of Jenghiz Khan: but even as the Varangian Confederacy was dissolving, a few hundred Norman knights led by the twelve sons of Tancred of Hauteville were snatching southern Italy from the Greeks and crossing the sea to oust the Saracens from Sicily, drive the Turks from Antioch, and mount a new, nominally Catholic, challenge to Byzantium. In Sicily they ruled a society at least as cosmopolitan as any improvised on the run by the pirates of the Caribbean and the Indian Ocean, and infinitely more luscious and civilized. Among the orange groves of Palermo, Roger I, making the best of several worlds, sat on his throne robed in the dalmatic of an apostolic delegate and the imperial costume of Byzantium, and enjoyed the amenities of a harem guarded by Nubian eunuchs.

The Viking saga, conceived in piracy but scattering colonies and dynasties in England, Ireland, Russia, France, Italy and Iceland, was followed by four or five centuries barren of any major piratical interest. The Viking surge had dwindled or been absorbed, the Viking spirit was dormant, most of all perhaps in Norway, Sweden and Denmark. The domes of Kiev glittered, the cathedrals of Monreale, Caen and Durham bore witness to the power and glory of apparently reformed warriors; but in Scandinavia the remnants of the Viking aristocracy expended their energies in interminable feuds, while thralls scratched a meagre living from an unresponsive soil.

Piracy shrivelled to petty proportions. The narrow seas swarmed with French, Scottish, English, Welsh and Irish ships on perpetual reprisal, using grapnels and long poles fitted with knives to slash rigging. Wool, wine and fish were the main prizes. A few gleams of style shine through this murky mêlée. Eustace the Monk, who left the cloister to join the private army of the Count of Boulogne, took to the seas after being outlawed for murder and established a reputation as a 'master pirate'. Rumour ran that the Black Monk was in league with the Devil and so could make his ship invisible. Selling his services to King John, he assembled a fleet that scoured the Channel and plundered up the Seine to Paris. He lived like a lord in a palace in London until, in 1212, King Philip of France offered him more attractive terms. Five years later he led a powerful fleet gathered for the invasion of England and was defeated off Sandwich by his former cronies from the Cinque Ports: manoeuvring to windward they showered Eustace's armada with eye-scorching clouds of powdered lime. Stuck on a lance, the Black Monk's head was paraded round southern England, while itinerant friars preached edifying sermons on the theme that all inveterate evil-doers come to a bad end.

William Marsh, exiled from the court of Henry III in 1235 for murder, was one of a long succession of freebooters who used Lundy Island in the Bristol Channel as their base. At its peak, his fleet operated from the Mull of Galloway to Land's End. Showing an aristocratic disdain for miscellaneous cargoes, he concentrated on kidnapping merchants in transit, who were kept in a dungeon on Lundy until their ransoms were paid. A popular figure, Marsh enhanced his notoriety when he tried to assassinate the King at Woodstock. But in 1242 his island stronghold was stormed. Imprisoned in the Tower of London, he and his principal lieutenants were hanged and their corpses dragged through the streets to be gibbeted.

In the last decade of the fourteenth century Stertebeker, a ruined and alcoholic German noble (his name signifies 'a beaker at one gulp'), in alliance with an outlaw known as Manteufel ('man-devil'), left the employ of the Hanseatic league to form a pirate confederacy which terrorized the Baltic and in 1392 sacked Bergen, the capital of Norway, and held its merchants to ransom. As with William Marsh, there was a certain aristocratic, even Robin Hood-ish, style about Stertebeker: a point that he seems to have stressed by calling his gang 'The Friends of God and Enemies of the World'. Two expeditions, the first equipped by Queen Margaret of Sweden and King Richard II of England, the second financed by the Hansa towns, failed to bring him to book. Not until 1402 was Stertebeker taken and executed. The story goes that the mainmast of his ship had a core of molten gold, so that the burgesses of Hamburg were able to recoup the costs of the expedition, recover the value of their lost cargoes, and donate a chunk of Stertebeker's spar to be fashioned into a golden crown of thanksgiving for the spire of the church of St Nicholas.

The beheading of Eustace the Black Monk, the most spectacular pirate of the early Middle Ages.

The clash of French and English corsairs produced some massive raids, as when, in 1399, John Hawley of Dartmouth (mayor, MP, and later Admiral of the West) captured thirty-four Norman and Breton vessels. The main item of plunder was 1,500 tuns of wine, some of which was set aside for a marathon public celebration: 'many puncheons of good Porto wine were broached . . . so that there was scarcely a sober man in the town, and for days no one thought of business or anything save eating, drinking and Merry-making'.

The exploits of Harry Pay of Poole had an audacity which raised them above the level of routine. In 1406 his ship was captured after a hand-to-hand fight off the Norman coast. Minutes before they were due for summary execution, Pay and his men overpowered and massacred their captors. Posing as master of the ship, the Dorset rover sailed up the Seine flying the French flag and made a devastating surprise attack on craft moored in the river. The Spaniards knew him as 'Arripay', and one official reported that 'he came often upon the coast of Castile and scoured the Channel by Flanders so powerfully that no vessel could pass that way without being taken. He burnt Gijon and carried off the crucifix from Santa Maria de Finisterre which was famous for its holiness. Much more damage Arripay did, taking more prizes and exacting ransoms. Although other armed ships came from England in like manner, he it was who came most often.' The Spaniards singled out Poole for reprisal. Choosing the time when Pay was burning, killing and looting his way up the Seine under false colours, Pedro Niño, the most celebrated Castilian corsair of the time, devastated the town so thoroughly that it never recovered its former commercial importance.

No doggerel or ballad commemorating these deeds has survived. That honour was reserved for Andrew Barton, a Scottish merchant who sailed on reprisal in 1511. Thirty-five years earlier, his father had been granted a letter of marque after his ships had been robbed by Portuguese pirates. Now his sons, Andrew, Robert and John, acted upon it. With two well-armed vessels, the *Lion* and the *Jennet Purwyn*, they plundered indiscriminately off the Flemish coast. Some of their prizes were Portuguese, a good many English. An early version of the ballad, in which Andrew Barton becomes Sir Andrew (a heroic figure whose countenance in death looks so noble that even his enemies mourn him), tells how King Henry VIII sends the Earl of Surrey's sons to 'reason' with the Bartons:

Fight on my men Sir Andrew says,
A little I'm hurt but yet not slain,
I'll but lie down and bleed a while,
And then I'll rise and fight again . . .

Later variations show the Barton brothers casting dice to decide which of them shall turn pirate to retrieve the family fortunes:

A Viking ship of the kind which terrorized the coasts of western Europe in the ninth century, from a ceiling painting in the church of Skamstrup, Denmark.

The body of William Marsh of Lundy dragged through the streets to be gibbeted, from the Chronicle *of the thirteenth-century historian Matthew Paris.*

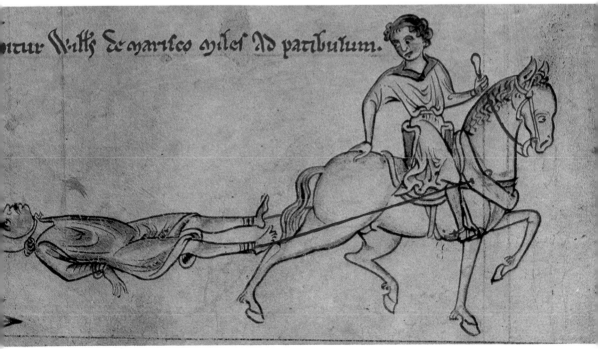

ntur Wills de marisco miles ad patibulum.

The Armada: even this most famous of naval engagements was fought by privateers who combined the national interest with plunder for private gain.

There were three brothers in merry Scotland,
In merry Scotland there were three,
And each of these brothers they did cast lots
To see which would rob the salt sea.

Henry, the youngest (upgraded to Sir Henry with his surname corrupted to 'Martyn'), is chosen:

Now lower your topsails you aldermen bold,
Come lower them under my lee,
Seeing I am resolved to pirate you here
To maintain my two brothers and me . . .

Bad news, bad news, to England has come,
Bad news I will tell to you all,
'Twas a rich merchant ship to England was bound
And most of her merry men drowned.

   Almost every subsequent pirate ballad in English derives from the Barton–Martyn cycle. The celebrated taunt –

Go home, go home, says Andrew Barton,
And tell your King from me
That he may reign king of the dry land
But I will be king of the sea

– was credited to John Ward and Peter Eston, star pirates in the Mediterranean nearly a century later.

In England almost all ranks of society began to have an interest in 'the sweet trade'. By the middle of the sixteenth century few fishermen were left in Rye, Hastings, Poole, Dartmouth or Fowey. Women took their places at the nets – 'eight or nine of them, with but one boy or man . . . a-fishing twenty or sixty miles to sea'. They might almost have spared their pains, for the markets were glutted with contraband fish. Monasteries and convents recently vacated by monks and nuns were filled with stolen goods. In the City of London the Austin Friars was stacked with dried cod and herring, the Grey Friars with barrels of wine, the Black Friars with prunes and figs. Loot was taken along the Thames by wherry to the water-stairs along the Strand, then by cart to the backyards of aldermen's residences. In taverns, chests were stowed in cellars, bales and barrels in stables, and churchyards were used as temporary burial-places. Along the south coast rovers openly displayed their wares on deck. Local gentry and clergy, farmers and shopkeepers, came from miles around to look them over – as when Bartholomew Brewton sailed into Lulworth, his pinnace crammed with velvets, silks and quality cloth taken from a Flemish ship off the North Foreland. To whet customers' appetites, Brewton, like other captains in a hurry, threatened to take his goods elsewhere – to Milford Haven perhaps, or Guernsey or the Isle of Man – if Dorset folk were not interested.

The methods of these rovers were more ruthless by far than those of Blackbeard and other reputed villains of the classical age of piracy. The crews of two Breton hoys captured by Cornish pirates off the Scillies in 1540 were murdered in cold blood. 'Captain Owen called to Philip the Welshman', deposed a witness later, 'and the said Philip called up the Bretons and caused John the mariner of Weymouth to bind their hands on cross behind their back. . . . They were drowned with their jerkins on about four leagues from land.' A Plymouth captain left a Spanish crew under hatches for forty-eight hours without food or drink while their cargo was ransacked, and finally locked them in the breadhouse, where 'they had no space to stand nor sit, but did lie upon one another like dogs, fast bound with cords'. English and Scottish pirates tortured prisoners by tying bow-strings round their wrists and 'privy members', and sometimes sliced off their ears and noses before drowning them. It was all a very far cry from the chivalrous tableau of the Andrew Barton ballad.

Since both Spain and Portugal used Antwerp as the main port for distributing cargoes throughout northern and central Europe, their ships had to run the gauntlet of the Channel. Not a trick was missed, and nothing was sacred. In 1548 Kentish rovers plundered a vessel containing the baggage of the Portuguese ambassador to France. In 1560 the Spanish ambassador in London protested that captured Spanish merchants had been put up to public auction at Dover and knocked down to purchasers who paid up to £100 apiece in the hope of making as much again in ransom.

William Hawkins, Sir Richard Grenville, and Thomas Cobham (the son of Lord Cobham, Warden of the Cinque Ports), among others, appeared before the Privy Council on charges of piracy, but received nothing but a reprimand for the sake of diplomatic appearances. The Principality of Wales was virtually a pirate domain. John Callice, an ex-haberdasher's apprentice from Tintern in Monmouthshire, was an acknowledged virtuoso, plundering freely in the Bristol Channel, around the Scillies, off the coast of East Anglia, and right up to Scotland. Rovers from England, Portugal and France came to Cardiff and Milford Haven, where the Earl of Pembroke and Sir John Perrot (the son of Henry VIII and Mary Berkeley) made sure that there was no interference. Officials did not dare to take any action, but, in the words of a frustrated Admiralty Court judge, 'play bo-peep, seest me, seest me not'. In North Wales, Vice-Admiral Sir Richard Bulkeley of Beaumaris frequently entertained pirates of several nationalities in his house. Bardsey Island was ruled by John Wyn ap Hugh, who used the former Augustinian Priory as a depot and ordered his lieutenants 'to be at all times ready to deliver to all such pirates victuals and necessaries, receiving for the same large recompense – as wine, iron, salt and spices'. Plunder

Lundy Island in the Bristol Channel, with its narrow-necked coves and steep cliffs, was for long a favourite base for English and Welsh pirates.

brought to Bardsey and Beaumaris was distributed to customers eighty miles inland, and a similar service was laid on from Cardiff and Milford Haven.

From Pendennis Castle at Falmouth Sir John Killigrew, Vice-Admiral of Cornwall and President of the Commissioners for Piracy, controlled a syndicate closely linked with the Welsh and Irish organizations. Powder and shot issued to the Killigrews to defend the coast against the threatened Spanish invasion was sold to pirate captains, and no vessel was safe from attack in Falmouth harbour. Sir John's mother led a boarding party which rifled a German ship and murdered several of the crew. His wife commanded a boatload of thugs in an assault on a Spanish merchantman driven into the harbour by a storm in 1582 – an act for which she was sentenced to death, but (unlike two of her employees) reprieved.

Though quayside taverns were the pirates' employment exchanges – the *George* at Billingsgate was a favourite signing-on point – crew members came not only from coastal areas but from towns and villages well inland. Often they included a number of Bretons or Hollanders, useful for their language and local knowledge. By the 1580s, when Callice made the first pirate cruise to the Mediterranean (he was killed in action off the Barbary coast), there might even be a few Turks, Moors and Africans.

Ashore, the pirates swaggered about in upper-class finery, peacocks of the streets and taverns who, as the chronicler John Stow grumbled, 'affect apparel too sumptuous for mere sea rovers'. When the gallows at Wapping *were* used, the crowds applauded the bravado of the condemned and clamoured for their gold rings and a share of their finery. In 1583, for instance, Thomas Walton and Clinton Atkinson were brought up from Corfe Castle in Dorset, the latter 'in murray velvet doublet with great gold buttons and Venetian velvet breeches laid with fresh gold lace', the former in breeches of crimson taffeta 'which he rent and distributed to such of his old acquaintances as stood about him'.

These bully-boys were apt to be transformed by death and legend into Robin Hoods. They might not give to the poor, but they did rob the rich of various countries, ape their manners, and wear their clothes. Round every pirate hanging eddied an undercurrent of class war.

The sea itself, in collaboration with the rocks and reefs of the Scillies, West Cornwall and North Devon, played Robin Hood or Pirate God to the scavenger communities of those fearful coasts. When wreckers' weather blew ('A savage sea and a shattering wind/The cliffs before and the gale behind'), whole villages assembled like vultures, with lanterns, axes, crowbars, carts, wheelbarrows and sacks, stalking a ship in distress and murdering survivors. 'We pray thee, O Lord,' petitioned the Scillonians, 'not that wrecks should happen, but that if any wrecks should happen, Thou wilt guide them to these Isles for the benefit of the inhabitants.'

Yet rich as the pickings were near home, the corsairs of Europe had, by the middle of the sixteenth century, begun to widen their scope. Piracy merged with imperialism in the contest for the riches of the New World, and the age of Drake was on the horizon.

The Caribbean and the South Sea

Chapter Three **Westward Ho!**

In August 1485 Christopher Columbus, a Genoese (or perhaps Corsican) pirate, fought under the French flag in a tremendous battle off Lisbon which resulted in an unprecedented haul of loot from Venetian galleys en route for England. But it was his epoch-making voyage to the Indies on behalf of the Catholic monarchs of Spain that changed the scope and style of piracy.

The French were the first to challenge the Iberian monopoly of Eldorado. In 1522 Giovanni da Verrazano, a Florentine in French pay, seized three Spanish ships, two laden with Mexican treasure and the other with sugar, hides and pearls from Hispaniola. By the 1530s French raiders were based in the Bahamas; and there, for the next two centuries, the innumerable cays (sandspits) provided ideal lurking-places for fast, predatory craft lying in wait for galleons beating out through the Florida Channel against the north-east trade wind.

The Spanish settlements in the West Indian islands – Cuba, Hispaniola, Puerto Rico – were sparsely garrisoned and minimally fortified. News of quicker fortunes to be made on the mainland as the *conquistadores* fought their way into the Inca Empire stripped the islands of colonists and relegated them to the status of ports of call for the treasure fleets. The mainland settlements – at Cartagena, Nombre de Dios, Vera Cruz, Panama – were for many years almost as vulnerable to determined plunderers. Local authorities warned Madrid that not one of the colonial centres could defend itself from attack by a few hundred resolute men. In 1537 the French raided Honduras and captured nine treasure ships. Seven years later they burned several defenceless settlements along the coast of New Granada (Venezuela). In quick succession came a systematic pillaging of Havana and Santiago de Cuba by François le Clerc (known to the Spaniards as Pie de Palo, or Peg Leg) and Jacques Sores.

Spain met the threat to the treasure fleets by a system of armed convoys. The itinerary, composition, and sailing dates of the great fleet which left Seville each spring was prescribed in minute detail. After arrival at Martinique it split, half going to the Isthmus of Darien (Panama), half to Mexico, to rejoin in late summer at Havana for the return voyage via the Azores. Outward bound the ships carried taffetas and silks, wine from Andalusia, and swords and armour of Toledo steel. Coming back they brought West Indian sugar and hides, cocoa and tobacco; gold and silver bullion from Peru, Mexico and Chile; emeralds from New Granada; pearls from Margarita and Rio de la Hacha; and spices, silks, jewels and gold

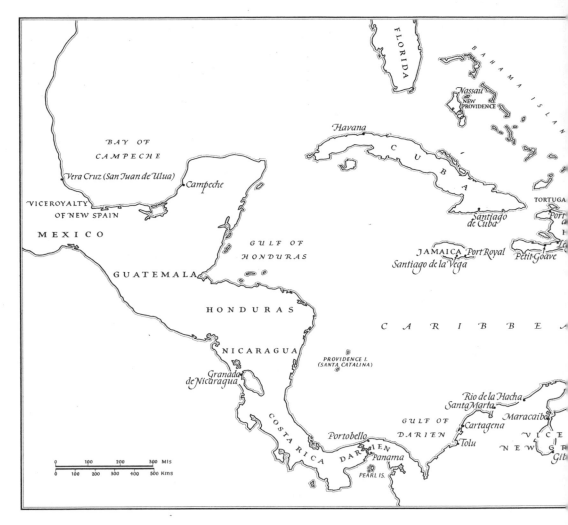

FLORIDA

BAHAMA ISLANDS

Havana

Nassau
NEW PROVIDENCE

BAY OF
CAMPECHE

C U B A

Vera Cruz (San Juan de Ulua)

Campeche

TORTUGA

VICEROYALTY
OF NEW SPAIN

*Santiago
de Cuba*

Port
a
H

MEXICO

GULF OF
HONDURAS

JAMAICA *Port Royal*   *Petit-Goave*
Santiago de la Vega

GUATEMALA

HONDURAS

C A R I B B E A

NICARAGUA

PROVIDENCE I.
(SANTA CATALINA)

*Granada
de Nicaragua*

Rio de la Hacha
Santa Marta
Maracaibo

GULF OF
DARIEN
Cartagena

C O S T A   R I C A

Portobello

DARIEN
Panama

Tolu

V I C E
N E W   G R
Gib

PEARL IS.

```
0        100       200      300 Mls
0    100   200   300   400   500 Kms
```

fetched from the Orient by the Manila galleons, unloaded at
Acapulco on the Pacific coast, and mule-packed to Vera Cruz. From
1580, when the crowns of Spain and Portugal were united, the
Spanish American take included sugar, hides, indigo, cotton and
timber from Brazil. But there was almost no naval defence except
when the *flotas* were in the Caribbean.

The English were slow to enter the Caribbean contest: the French
actually taunted them for their 'sluggish security'. Yet, galled by the
harsh fines, confiscations and occasional execution as heretics to
which merchants and mariners were subjected after the break with
Rome, they were groping towards similar conclusions. In 1545
Robert Reneger of Southampton surprised the *San Salvador*,
homeward bound from Hispaniola with a cargo of gold, sugar and
hides, off Cape St Vincent. He proposed to take only the value of
some prizes of his impounded by the Spaniards, and to give the
captain a certificate to that effect. The captain, however, begged

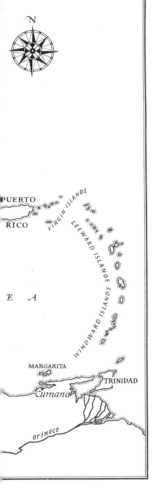

N

PUERTO
RICO

VIRGIN ISLANDS

LEEWARD ISLANDS

WINDWARD ISLANDS

E A

MARGARITA

TRINIDAD

Cumana

orinoco

The Caribbean, showing chief pirate strongholds and targets from the sixteenth to the eighteenth century.

Reneger not to mention the gold, since it was being smuggled into Spain as a private venture. After a flurry of diplomatic notes and the payment of dues to Henry VIII and the Lord Admiral, Reneger retired, the sixteenth-century equivalent of a millionaire, to become Collector of Customs in Southampton.

Reneger's exploit encouraged a concerted attack on Spanish and Portuguese vessels returning from the Indies and the Guinea Coast, with Baltimore in Ireland becoming a busy centre for the disposal of cargoes of gold, ivory, spices, silk, sugar and hides. The brief interlude of counter-reformation under Mary Tudor, the wife of Philip II of Spain, could not halt this process, now regarded as part of a war of religion and national survival. *Nouveau riche* nobles and merchants had too great a stake in Protestantism to be deflected from the course of plunder. The Tremaynes and the Killigrews, powerful bosses of West Country pirate syndicates, continued their private war with French commissions. By the 1560s the emergence of Spain as a super-power forced Protestant rulers to give at least semi-official sanction to these syndicates and their French (Huguenot) and Dutch counterparts. The King of Spain was also Lord of Burgundy, Archduke of Milan, King of Naples, and monarch of an empire stretching from the Philippines to the Caribbean, from the Straits of Magellan to the coast of California.

Between 1568 and 1572, as French and Dutch Protestant privateers, based on La Rochelle and Dover, co-operated with the English syndicates, the corsair operation became increasingly complex. English pirates bought commissions from Henry of Navarre to attack French Catholic shipping. The *Castle of Comfort*, armed and commanded by Thomas Jones, a gentleman of Lynn, and victualled by a London merchant, was licensed by the Huguenot Admiral Coligny. Later it was hired to a French captain with connections in the Isle of Wight (a noted pirate centre and plunder mart) under licence from the Prince de Condé, and cruised off Morocco and in the Caribbean.

So far, English enterprise in the Caribbean itself had been confined to the slave-smuggling of John Hawkins, patron of Drake and later Treasurer and designer-in-chief to the infant Royal Navy. The profits of his first two cruises were spectacular as he bartered West African Negroes for gold, sugar and hides. Indeed, this was a far more effective method of draining the wealth of the Indies than the more violent techniques of Pie de Palo, Jacques Sores and the burglars of the Bahamas, so soon to be imitated by Drake. But the débâcle which completed the failure of Hawkins's already disastrous third venture put an end to the idea of bribing rather than blasting a way to a place in the Caribbean sun. Hawkins's ships, battered by a tropical storm, were forced to shelter at San Juan de Ulua shortly before the *flota* from Seville, with the new Viceroy, Don Martín Enriquez, sailed into the harbour. What followed was, according to one's point of view, an act of foul treachery or a long-overdue lesson

43

to heretical trespassers and backsliding colonists that the rules were not to be flouted with impunity. Don Martín, a zealous newcomer, gave Hawkins a written guarantee not to molest his squadron, then ordered a surprise attack upon it. Only Hawkins in the *Minion* and young Francis Drake in the fifty-ton *Judith* escaped to tell the tale.

Of course it was a tale of unmitigated papist duplicity, spiced and sharpened by the fanaticism of Drake, who had been reared in a bitterly anti-papist home and whose favourite reading was Foxe's *Book of Martyrs*. In 1572, with financial backing from Hawkins, he sailed to the Isthmus of Darien with two tiny ships and seventy-one men bent on gold, glory and revenge – and inaugurated a new phase in English piracy. Four prefabricated pinnaces were assembled in a hidden anchorage for a night attack on Nombre de Dios, but the treasure depots were empty. The pirates had to wait for nearly a year until the *flota* was in harbour. An overland trek through dense jungle to ambush mule-trains from Panama, though helped by the expertise of Indian tribesmen and *cimarrones* (escaped Negro and Indian slaves) who shared Drake's thirst for vengeance, failed when a drunken sailor alerted the convoy. Two weeks later, when all seemed lost, the Englishmen's luck turned with the capture of a train stacked with gold and silver. Half his men, including his brothers, had died of yellow fever and jungle sores, but the voyage was 'made', Drake exultantly announced, 'drawing a quoit of gold from his bosom' (as Richard Hakluyt, the great chronicler of Elizabethan expansion, puts it), when he and the survivors got back to the hidden ships after a six-hour drift downriver on a raft up to their waists in water.

When in 1580, at the end of Drake's second voyage, the *Golden Hind* sailed up the Thames after circumnavigating the globe, she left behind a trail of unparalleled plunder. The terrible passage through the Straits of Magellan and the seven-thousand-mile crossing of the Pacific to the Spice Isles had been tough, but the ravaging of the coasts and shipping of Chile and Peru, and the capture of the *Cacafuego*, a Manila galleon containing 'thirteen chests full of reals of plate, four score pound weight of gold, and six and twenty tons of silver', were child's play. The Spaniards, by now resigned to the hazards of the Caribbean, were totally unprepared for attack from the rear. Even after jettisoning half his loot to keep the ship afloat, Drake came through with a 4,700 per cent profit.

His Caribbean cruises of 1585 and 1595 were cumbersome operations, destructive but financially unsuccessful. Drake the west-country squire, mayor of Plymouth and national hero, could not repeat the fierce loner joy of the 1570s. Through all the spectacular daring, the exotic landfalls, the tight corners and the encounters with strange tribes, he remained a local rover made good. The outlaw element was lacking. However tight-stretched, the ties that bound him to the givers of approval and knighthoods never broke. He was no spendthrift either, and worked hard to present himself as the God-fearing, courteous Protestant knight-errant of the seas. But Drake's

Silver from the mines at Potosí, Peru, was among the prizes which pirates hoped to snatch from the Spanish treasure fleets.

.SVR.

PONIENTE

Tollocsi

hornos donde gustavan la mas

prayers ('O Lord, make us rich, for we must have gold before we see England') closely resemble those of the Varangians as they knelt before their idols on the banks of the Volga. He bought his way up the established social ladder, marrying as his second wife a former royal maid of honour, and acquiring Buckland Abbey from the Grenvilles, who had purchased it from the Crown at the time of the dissolution of the monasteries. Here, in a Protestant pirate's apotheosis, he kept his own court, including a tame papist refugee, Dom Antonio, pretender to the throne of Portugal, who sold jewels and privateering licences to his heretic protector.

Henry Robarts, also a Devon man and sailor, commended the Elizabethan corsairs in some doggerel published in 1595:

Drake encounters Indian tribesmen at the River Plate on the epoch-making voyage of the Golden Hind (1577–80).

'Tis England's honour that you have in hand
Then think thereof if you do love our land.
The gain is yours if millions home you bring,
Then courage take, to gain so sweet a thing . . .
And for my part I wish you always health,
With quick return and so much store of wealth
That Philip's regions may not more be stored
With pearls and jewels and the purest gold. . . .

But though between 1585 and 1603, when war with Spain, not formally declared, was as total as the corsairs could make it, hundreds of private ventures were financed, venturers did not fling their booty around with the open-handedness of John Hawley and his like. Oceanic cruises demanded long purses and shrewd accounting. As Drake himself had discovered, there was an increasing tendency for pirate captains to become employees of the money-lenders, and above all of the magnates of the City of London – merchant capitalists for whom piracy meant the carrying on of commerce by other means, and who were not inclined to waste their dividends on public junketing. Hawkins's improvements in armament and ship design, the expertise of Drake and his contemporaries, were harnessed to the demands of the new long-distance trading combines, in particular the East India Company.

James Lancaster, whose daring raid of 1595 on the port of Pernambuco in Brazil netted a fabulous tally of silks, jewels, spices, indigo and calicoes, was by 1600 a prominent Company shareholder and sea captain, together with such experienced masters of 'reprisal' in the Caribbean as Christopher Newport and William Parker. They were instructed to take prizes whenever this could be contrived 'without prejudice or hazard of the voyage' – that is, when greater speed and fire-power made it a safe bet. After seizing a number of Portuguese cargoes in the Malacca Straits on his first voyage for the Company, Lancaster, with true puritan piety, wrote in his journal: 'Praise be to God. He hath not only supplied my necessities to lade these ships I have, but hath given me as much as would lade many more if I had them.'

In the three years following the defeat of the Spanish Armada, privateering returns were at least as great as those of the legitimate pre-war Iberian trade. The Brazil trade was so heavily hit that London was glutted with sugar and hides (one merchant renamed his ship the *Sugar*) and vessels were re-routed north of Scotland to Hamburg in an attempt to reduce losses. Not surprisingly, there was

a rush of gentleman adventurers, including the Earls of Essex and Cumberland and Sir Walter Raleigh. Most of them were deeply in debt and, in the words of a vivid phrase of the time, 'threw their lands into the sea' in the hope of a tremendous dividend.

Glory-mongering and reckless competition for royal favour did not make for prudence. Voyages were planned on such an ambitious scale, and eager amateurs were so roundly cheated by victuallers and other tradesmen, that resounding ruin was the usual result. Some, like Edward Glenham of Benhall in Suffolk (who sold his family seat to attempt the capture of St George's Island in the Azores), or the Sherley brothers (who vainly sought a quick killing in the Gulf of Guinea, the Caribbean and the Mediterranean), were forced in sheer desperation to drop all pretence of legality. Raleigh, who failed in a gold-hunt along the Orinoco, spoke for all of them in his haughty reply to a rebuke from the moralizing Francis Bacon: 'Did you know of any that were pirates for millions? They only that work for small things are pirates.'

Thomas Cavendish, a Suffolk squire who, at colossal expense, managed to save the honour of the gentlemen by repeating Drake's feat of 1577–80, was, like Drake, knighted on his return. His voyage was undertaken in time of open war, and its success was judged as much by its sheer destructiveness as by its profitability. When Cavendish took the great Manila galleon, the *Santa Ana*, off the coast of California, he set fire to it with five hundred tons of costly cargo aboard. 'Along the coasts of Chile, Peru and New Spain', he wrote in a report to his patron, Lord Hunsdon, 'I made great spoils. I burnt and sunk nineteen ships, both great and small. All the villages and towns that I landed at, I burnt and spoiled.'

If the Drake of the 1570s was the patron saint or unattainable ideal of the big-time buccaneers of the seventeenth century, Cavendish was their working model: and he seemed a triumphant exception to the rule of amateur incompetence. The progress of his aptly named flagship, the *Desire*, up the Thames in 1588 was a masterpiece of pirate-jingo bravado – the bows shining with gilt, the topmasts wrapped in cloth of gold, the sails of multicoloured silk-grass from the South Sea islands, Cavendish and his sea-dogs strutting on deck in magnificent silks and brocades. His booty was vast but soon dissipated at court or mopped up by creditors. When he fitted out his second expedition in 1591, Cavendish again had to sell or mortgage manors. This time his luck was out, and he died at sea, cursing the 'insolent, mutinous mariners' who in his view had ruined the voyage.

Drake was one of the few Elizabethan corsair captains to keep his crew well under control, perhaps not without recourse to such punishments as cutting off a hand (for drawing a knife on an officer), ducking three times from the yard-arm (for assaulting a shipmate), shaving the head and smearing it with a mixture of feathers and boiling oil (for stealing), flogging or marooning (for falling asleep on

Sir John Hawkins, slave-trader, pirate and naval architect : the nimble, heavily-gunned ships he designed helped to rout the Spanish Armada.

watch, blaspheming at cards or dice, or 'filthy talk at mess'). During the long piratical orgy of the Spanish War, seasoned mariners were in a strong position. Knowing that they were in steep demand, they became less and less inclined to put up with harsh discipline. Richard Hawkins* described them as 'like to a stiff-necked horse which, taking the bridle between his teeth, forceth his rider to do what him list.' By the 1590s it was normal practice to consult the crew in any important matter, and they often compelled a captain to change the course and objectives of a voyage.

Even before 1585, serving men and apprentices from farms and towns around the coast from Bristol to the Wash had run away to go on the account, 'openly saying that why should they serve for forty shillings a year when they might make their share at sea within a week'. This did not include what they might add in pillage and embezzlement: for sailors who risked their health and their lives in filthy, overcrowded conditions (the number of men was calculated on the need for prize crews and the certainty of many deaths from dysentery, scurvy and gangrene) did not stick too scrupulously to the terms of their privateering contract. The crews' third of the value of prize goods was at the mercy of the promoters' arithmetic. The temptation to 'break bulk' – pilfer from a cargo before it was officially inventoried and divided – was strong and often not resisted. When William Ivey, master of the *Tiger*, a London-financed privateer, was reproved for 'making spoil of the goods', he said 'shite on thy commissions' and, together with the master's mate and the quarter-master, knifed the captain (who had given bond not to permit pilfering) and threatened to throw him overboard.

Pillage was a cause of endless strife. It meant the traditional right of a victorious crew to take possession of goods and valuables not belonging to the cargo proper. These included most items found above deck, and the personal effects of crews and passengers. Every man was supposed to bring what he found to the mainmast, where it would be shared according to rank, the chief officers being entitled to certain specified perquisites in addition to their fixed quota; but in the heat of the moment of boarding, it was an easy step from pillage to rifling the cargo in the hold. A conscientious captain sometimes found it hard to decide which was worse for discipline, the failure to run down a rich prize or the taking of one.

Not many captains were conscientious, and the Crown, the Lord Admiral, and the promoters were systematically cheated. A large proportion of prize goods was smuggled ashore in England, Wales, or Ireland, and sometimes disposed of at Algiers or Tunis. Shrewd merchants operating an extensive black market made enormous profits by buying at rock-bottom prices, but most of the mariners' hot money went on drink and whores.

* Sir Richard Hawkins (1560–1622), only son of Sir John, was in 1608 arrested and fined for condoning piracy. He was Vice-Admiral of Devon at the time.

Thomas Cavendish and crew slay sea-lions and are attacked by natives during his marathon pirate cruise of 1586–8.

The turning of a blind eye was reckoned a patriotic virtue. Sir George Carey, a prominent businessman, reasoned that 'Her Majesty shall not need to espy the faults of those who will venture to do her service', and financed a cruise by 'one Flud, a valiant and skilful pirate weary, as he protesteth, of his former trade'. Many promoters did not bother to get commissions, confident that they could buy their way out of any trouble.

'How just is the hatred which all peoples bear to the English', wrote Giovanni Scaramelli, the Venetian ambassador, in a despatch of 20 March 1603 to the Doge and Senate, 'for they are the disturbers of the whole world. And yet they not only do not take any steps to remedy the mischief, but glory that the English name should become formidable in just this way. The Queen's ships do not amount to more than fifteen or sixteen and her revenue cannot support a greater charge; and so the whole strength and repute of the nation rests on the vast number of small corsairs. They make the politicians partners in their profits, without the risk of a penny in the fitting out, but only a share in the prizes, which are adjudged by legal creatures appointed by the politicians themselves. To such a state has this unhappy kingdom come, that from a lofty religion has fallen into the abyss of infidelity.'

The foundation of many a Roundhead fortune was laid in those days. Yet piracy – or privateering – drew people of many conditions into a common enterprise combining the thrills of plunder with patriotism. Everyone who had a few shillings to spare put them into a venture. If the merchants and gentleman plunderers sometimes struck lucky, they also took some hard knocks, and upper-class corsairs had to haul and draw with the rest. Pirate democracy, in fact, gave satisfaction at many levels, and from it blew a rebellious gust that helped to sweep away the divine right of kings and whistled in the words of Thomas Rainborowe: 'the poorest he that is in England hath a life to live as the greatest he.'

Nicholas Hilliard's portrait of the Earl of Cumberland, one of the 'amateur' privateers who tried to emulate Drake's lucrative exploits.

The French raids in the Caribbean, and Francis Drake's plundering on the Isthmus and in the South Sea (Pacific), had set the new pattern of piracy. The distinction of pioneering a short cut to the South Sea, however, went to John Oxenham, the hero of Charles Kingsley's *Westward Ho!* Oxenham, who came from a well-to-do Devon family, had shared the tribulations and the glory of the Nombre de Dios coup as Drake's lieutenant (and probably helped to finance the expedition). In 1574 he fitted out his own venture, returning to the secret anchorage in the Gulf of Darien with a crew of seventy in a ship of 140 tons.

His old acquaintances, the *cimarrones*, told him that the mule trains were now too strongly guarded for there to be much hope of a successful ambush. Oxenham decided to 'do that which never any man before enterprised'. His ship, the topmasts struck and camouflaged with branches, was beached among the trees bordering the shore and left under a guard of four or five men. The rest went off into the jungle far inland. There they constructed a forty-five-foot-long pinnace and, travelling downstream, eventually reached the Pacific coast. In the Pearl Islands, two treasure ships from Lima were taken and rifled, and the voyage made. But owing to Oxenham's generosity in allowing the ships to go on their way to Panama, the pinnace was pursued and all the company killed or captured. The mariners were shot in Panama, while Oxenham was sent to Lima and hanged as a pirate in the main square – a picturesque loser, but also a pathfinder for the buccaneer armies to come.

Chapter Four Bloody, Bloody Buccaneer

Since the 1530s, successive waves of privateers and smugglers had deposited French, English, Dutch and Portuguese deserters and maroons on the coasts of Cuba, Jamaica and Hispaniola, but especially along the north-west shore of Hispaniola. Here the savannahs abounded in wild pigs and cattle which had escaped the periodic roundups and multiplied prodigiously. From the few surviving Indians the European dropouts learned the art of the *boucan*, the curing of long strips of meat on a barbecue over a slow fire of dung and wood-chips. Before long they were doing a good trade with interlopers, selling smoked meat, hides, and tallow (used to coat hulls as a protection against the teredo worm).*

In exchange they took gunpowder, lead bullets, muskets (preferably long-barrelled muzzle-loaders from Nantes or Bordeaux), cloth, provisions, brandy and rum. Small, remote Spanish settlements took part in the boom, and runaway slaves found the butchers' roving life preferable to the miseries of the plantations.

The *boucaniers* began to style themselves 'Brethren of the Coast', and evolved their own peculiar life-style. Few questions were asked, the past was erased, the hunters rechristened with nicknames. They hunted in pairs or small bands, and got to be such crack marksmen that they could hit a spun coin in mid-air. Sharpshooting, drinking – they invented a mixture of rum and gunpowder that was to be the he-man pirate's compulsory tipple – and gambling were their main diversions, the warm marrow from the bones of freshly slaughtered beasts their favourite food. Festooned with hatchets, skinning-

---

* Weed (which made them slow and hard to steer) and marine borers were a constant menace to wooden ships in warm tropical waters. The most common borers were the soft-shelled teredos, molluscs rather than worms, equipped with fine saw-teeth. They entered the planking through minute holes, then bored parallel to the surface as they grew. Able to lay about a million eggs a year, they could honeycomb a hull on a long voyage. Other borers devoured the planking from outside, layer by layer. To counteract this ships were double-planked, with a layer of felt and tar between, and were careened as often as possible, at least every two to three months. Careening was a longish and tedious business, and one which laid a crew open to attack. Guns and stores were taken out, and the guns mounted on improvised earthworks commanding the entrance to a bay, while the ship was beached and tilted over and its bottom scraped, smeared with tallow and pitch, and patched. Early experiments in lead-sheathing failed because the galvanic action of lead on iron nails and hoops ate the metal away. When they could afford to, buccaneers preferred to have their barques and brigantines built of worm-resisting cedarwood from the Bermudas. Extraordinary expedients were tried in leaky, worm-eaten ships, as when Prince Rupert's crew, battered and sinking off the Azores in 1651, trod strips of raw beef between started timbers.

This typically dramatic painting by Howard Pyle, the American illustrator, shows buccaneers extorting booty from the inhabitants of a captured Spanish town.

55

knives, powder-horns and bullet-bags, and with mosquito nets coiled round their waists for nights spent in the open, they wore peaked, short-brimmed hats, linen shirts caked with blood, and stinking, uncured rawhide trousers and boots. All in all, they looked and lived like savages.

Punitive expeditions failed to scare them off, and they began to alternate their butcher's trade with attacks on Spanish shipping made in *piraguas* (long canoes hollowed out from tree-trunks with fire and axe) or single-masted barques. Their technique was to pack a vessel with marksmen (on the principle that four muskets were as good as one cannon), manoeuvre so as to keep the bow towards their prey, thus presenting the smallest possible target, move in close under a barrage of accurate fire, jam the rudder, and swarm up the stern. Attempts to destroy the livelihood of the buccaneers by wholesale massacre of the herds intensified their turn for piracy. From about 1630 Tortuga, a short sea journey from the north-west coast of Hispaniola, became an alternative headquarters.

Meanwhile, the whole of the Caribbean was being heavily colonized from Europe. In 1555, with two small ships and about a hundred men, Jacques Sores had captured Havana and razed it to the ground. There was no naval defence, and only three dozen soldiers armed with swords and crossbows to oppose him. After a token resistance, the Governor retreated inland to join the rest of the

(Opposite)
The original buccaneers were hunters and butchers by trade, bartering hides, tallow and smoked meat for long-barrelled muskets, provisions, brandy and rum.

These details from a French map published in 1705 show (below) *the technique of the* boucan – *smoking of raw meat – which the original* boucaniers *learned from the Indians of Hispaniola, and* (right) *buccaneers swearing on the Bible not to cheat their fellow Brethren of the Coast in the share-out of booty.*

LES BOUCANNIERS. ou FLIBUSTIERS.

population (together with their cattle and more valuable possessions) and began ransom negotiations. These were prolonged in the hope of wearing out the raiders' patience and beating down the price of their departure: a tactic frequently used during the next 150 years, even after Spanish defences in the Caribbean had been strengthened.

Sores' achievement inspired a whole series of abortive French projects for a large-scale naval expedition that was to sack Santo Domingo (the capital of Hispaniola), sail on to the Isthmus, seize Panama and capture the South Sea fleet, intercept the Mexican *flota* and return home, having wrecked the economy and war potential of Spain. Drake and Cromwell had much the same ambition, but it was never fully realized – though in 1628 Piet Heyn, commanding the thirty-one-sail fleet of the Dutch West India Company, captured the entire homeward-bound *flota* almost without firing a shot. This coup ruined Spanish credit in Europe, yielded a 50 per cent dividend to Company shareholders, and helped to finance a vigorous Dutch trade offensive in Brazil.

After the rush to the mainland the Spanish islands – Cuba, Jamaica, Hispaniola, Puerto Rico – were left with tiny populations. Only key centres like Havana were (in time) adequately fortified. But the Caribbean stretched almost two thousand miles from west to east, and nearly a thousand from north to south at its widest. The hundreds of smaller islands which form a breakwater arc against the Atlantic, from the Bahamas in the north through the Virgin, Leeward and Windward Islands to Trinidad and Curaçao in the south, were wide open to 'trespassers'. Government was feeble and venal, and this was the wildest segment of the 'Wild West', a frontier region where ships instead of horses carried the sharpshooters.

Portobello, which in 1584 replaced Nombre de Dios as the point of lading for the treasure of Peru and Chile, typified a prevailing atmosphere of sleazy, brutal, almost casually murderous materialism. It came boisterously alive only during the four weeks of the great annual fair. Bars and bricks of silver and gold were stacked in the dirty streets alongside tethered mules as bullion, pearls and gems poured in to a present-day value of about £600 million. Travellers and merchants were charged fantastic prices for a verminous room in which to sleep or display their wares. Drunken brawls and yellow fever took a heavy toll. In 1637 more than five hundred men died of sickness while the fleet was in port. Reckless greed was stronger than the fear of pirates and hurricanes. The galleons and their armed escorts, often unwieldy in design, were made more cumbersome and vulnerable by being crammed with illicit merchandise and passengers. Undergunned and undermanned, it was all they could do to withstand bad weather, let alone fight off a determined attack.

The first French colony in Florida had been wiped out by the Spaniards in the sixteenth century. After that, the English, French and Dutch West India Companies concentrated on the Leeward and Windward Islands. They were small, easy to depopulate and

A soigné version of a late
seventeenth-century buccaneer
from P. Christian's Histoire des
Pirates (Paris, 1850).

repeople, and valued initially less for their economic potential as
tobacco- or sugar-producers than as corsair bases and smuggling
depots. Between 1625 and 1640 the Dutch grabbed Saba, St Martin,
St Eustatius and Curaçao; the English combined with the French to
seize St Kitts and with the Dutch to occupy St Croix, and took sole
possession of Barbados, Nevis, Antigua and Montserrat; the French
waged a war of extermination with the Caribs in Martinique and
Guadeloupe. The English settlements were planted by competing
groups of investors scrambling for patents and patronage in London.
Governments saw no reason to discourage the multiplication of
colonies which, like the activities of the corsairs, cost them nothing,
and which also provided dumping-grounds for felons, paupers and
schismatics.

The miserable condition of landless labourers made the offer of
free land in the West Indies – pictured as a kind of earthly paradise –
an attractive bait. Pauperized workers in France, England and
Holland flocked to start a new life on seven-year contracts as
indentured servants, with free passage and board and the prospect of
becoming landlords and employers themselves in due course. More
often than not, like Exquemelin, they found themselves bought and
sold, their contracts indefinitely prolonged on one pretext or

another; they might even be condemned to slavery on the plantations alongside Negroes and transportees. After Cromwell's victory in the English Civil War, the latter included political opponents, almost any Irishman, and seven thousand Scottish prisoners of war. Of the emigrants who were lucky enough to get a fair-minded master and acquire a smallholding, most were soon ruined by the sugar revolution. By the 1650s, sugar had become the only product of importance, and it was a rich man's crop demanding capital to invest in machinery and big plantations. Tobacco farmers and other smallholders were ruthlessly squeezed out, adding to the army of malcontents. When Captain William Jackson, armed with a privateering commission from the Earl of Warwick, arrived in the West Indies in 1642, he had no difficulty signing on more than a thousand men, mostly from St Kitts and Barbados, for a plunder cruise along the Spanish Main from Caracas to Honduras.

Ten years later, when Prince Rupert of the Rhine, a cavalry leader turned pirate, arrived with three ships to secure the British West Indian islands for his cousin in exile Prince Charles, he found them controlled by Cromwell's men: but French buccaneers were willing to do a deal with him until they discovered he had no money and was a most indifferent sailor. In 1655 nearly six thousand of the troops of Cromwell's armada, which failed to capture Hispaniola but just managed to seize Jamaica, were taken on at Barbados, Nevis and St Kitts. This Grand Design, as it was called, was solemnly justified as a religious duty by John Milton, Cromwell's learned Latin Secretary; but it was in effect a buccaneering expedition, undertaken without a declaration of war at a time when negotiations were in progress for an alliance with Spain. The picture on the other side was much the same: Spanish garrisons and the crews of Spanish coastguard squadrons were composed of mercenary toughs self-righteously but accurately described by an English Governor as 'a mongrel parcel of thieves and rogues that rob and murder all that come into their power without the least respect to humanity or common justice'.

The French, English and Dutch islands were full of desperadoes for whom the corsair life offered employment, a chance of quick and easy money, and the only kind of freedom they were ever likely to know. The men who became known as buccaneers or flibustiers (allegedly a French corruption of the word freebooter) were the rejects, the bohemian underside, of a viciously acquisitive society united only in its determination to murder the natives and rob the Spaniards. Often enough they acted as the hatchet-men of faraway Company directors and opportunistic governments, shifting gear from privateering to piracy and back again so often that the clutch of moral and legal distinction was worn away.

By 1650 Levasseur, the self-appointed 'Governor' of a heavily-fortified Tortuga, had brought the island, with its fine natural harbour, under French control. Levasseur was murdered, but his successors, notably the energetic Bertrand d'Ogéron, took over

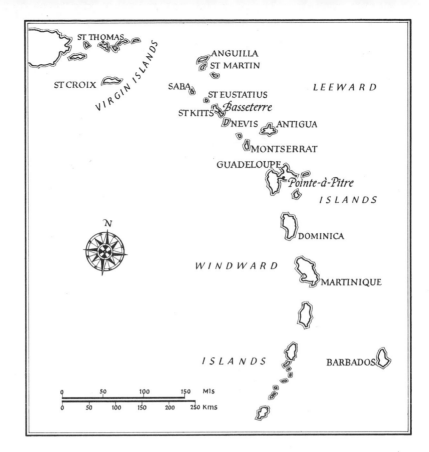

The Virgin, Leeward and Windward Islands.

(Overleaf) *In 1628 the Dutch West India squadron, seen here in action off Havana, captured the entire Spanish treasure fleet – the most sensational coup in a relentless trade war fought largely by seasoned pirates.*

Tortuga for the French West India Company and extended their rule to the buccaneer colonies in Hispaniola, importing hundreds of prostitutes in an effort to domesticate and heterosexualize their ruffian subjects. After the English occupation of Jamaica, Port Royal became a rival buccaneering base, and the Brotherhood of the Coasts began to suffer strain as England, France and Holland entered a period of intense colonial rivalry. During the 1690s flibustiers from Tortuga, and from Petit-Goave, Léogane and Port-de-Paix (the harbours of French Hispaniola or Saint-Domingue, later Haiti), carried off so many slaves in raids on Jamaica that they mockingly referred to the island as Little Guinea. But the buccaneers were awkward makeweights in the balance of power. When asked to fight the Dutch, French or English, their efforts tended to be half-hearted, and were often abandoned in favour of the time-honoured 'crusade' against the Spaniards, who after all still held the gold, silver and emerald mines and most of the pearl fisheries and offered far richer returns of plunder. During the sack of Cartagena in 1697 (a joint naval-flibustier operation), feeling ran so high about the division of the enormous booty that the two contingents of the French fleet almost fought each other – and the buccaneers returned to the city for a second round of extortion.

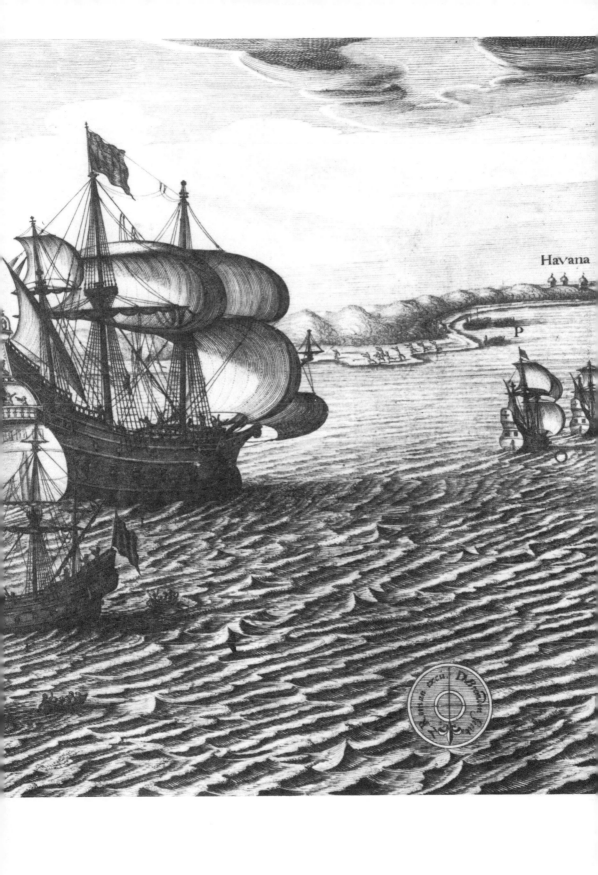

Havana

P

At its organized height, the age of the buccaneers lasted little more than thirty years, from 1665 to 1697. In the years before Lolonois, Mansfield, Morgan, Grammont and Laurens de Graaf began to marshal them in their thousands for a dully repetitive round of pillage, the improvising loners had their day. Among them were men like Louis le Golif, nicknamed Borgne-Fesse because one of his buttocks had been sliced off; Bâbord-Amure (known as 'Port Tack' because his nose had been smashed askew); Bartolomeo el Portugués, famous for bad luck as much as daring, who with thirty men in a leaking *piragua* took a twenty-gun Spanish brig off Cuba, made off with seventy thousand pieces of eight, was captured, but escaped by using two empty wine jars as floats (he could not swim); Roche Braziliano, a bear-like Dutchman who, according to Exquemelin, 'when drunk would roam about like a madman. The first person he came across he would chop off his arm or leg. . . . Some Spaniards he tied or spitted on wooden stakes and roast them alive – perhaps because they refused to show him the way to the hog-yards he wanted to plunder'; Montbars the Exterminator, a Frenchman from Languedoc who claimed that his sadistic treatment of Spaniards was motivated not only by their 'treacherous' attacks on the buccaneers in Hispaniola but by their fiendish cruelty to the Indians; 'Red Legs' Greaves, a Scottish transportee who escaped from Barbados and bought a plantation at Nevis on the proceeds of a fabulously successful raid on a Spanish pearling fleet off the island of Margarita; and Pierre le Grand, called 'the Great' after his capture of a treasure ship by night assault (he and his companions, maddened by hunger, thirst and exposure, deliberately holed their *piragua* to heighten their do-or-die mood).

Pierre, like Red Legs, got out quickly: he is said to have sailed his prize straight to Dieppe, his home town, where he died a rich and respected citizen. Few buccaneers were so lucky or so prudent. 'That is the way with them,' wrote Exquemelin. 'They don't keep their money for long. They are busy dicing, whoring and drinking so long as they have anything to spend. Some of them will get through a good 3,000 dollars in a day, and next day not have a shirt to their back, . . . spending with huge prodigality what others had gained with no small toil. My own master used to buy a butt of wine, set it in the middle of the street with the head stove in, and stand barring the way. Every passer-by had to drink with him or he'd have shot them dead with a gun he kept handy. Once he bought a cask of butter and threw the stuff at everyone who came by. . . . The tavern-keepers give credit, but will often sell you into slavery for debt. The man who gave the whore so much to see her stripped was sold like this by the very man in whose house he had spent thousands of dollars.'

The survivors of the Old Guard – far outnumbered by recent recruits who had never seen a *boucan* or shot it out with Spanish patrols in the woods and savannahs of Hispaniola – were the élite of the next phase, the phase of the Great Captains and the big battalions, when ships were little more than troop-transports on a shuttle service to the battered towns of the Isthmus and the Main. Time after time the Spaniards evacuated, hid their valuables, were tortured to reveal where the treasure was, and haggled over individual or collective ransoms. Time after time, with almost heroic resilience, they rebuilt their houses and resumed business as usual.

Land raids became the fashion because the success of Piet Heyn and the buccaneers had almost cleared the Caribbean of Spanish shipping other than the annual *flota*. Lewis Scot, sailing from Port Royal, led the way by plundering Campeche on the coast of Mexico and holding it to ransom. His example was quickly followed by John Davis, who with ninety men in three *piraguas* paddled forty leagues up river to loot Granada de Nicaragua; Edward Mansfield, who preceded Morgan as 'Admiral' or 'General' of the Port Royal buccaneers; and François Lolonois, so named after his birthplace in Brittany, Les Sables d'Olonne. Lolonois, according to Exquemelin, was a rip-roaring psychopath. One of the Old Guard, he had been shipped out as an indentured servant, escaped to Hispaniola, and emerged in Tortuga as the king of toughs. Such, indeed, was his reputation for ferocity that the citizens of Havana begged the Governor not to attempt retaliation against the buccaneers.

With Michel le Basque and about seven hundred men, Lolonois sacked Maracaibo and Gibraltar in New Granada, and later assembled a force of about a thousand for a regular campaign of plunder in Nicaragua. During these expeditions his savagery amazed even his most hardened followers, though it was probably little worse than the reprisals of the Spaniards – or the behaviour of freebooting armies during the Thirty Years War, or of Cromwell's troops in Ireland. Exquemelin shows him 'murdering ten or twelve Spaniards without turning a hair' in true slaughterhouse style, and claims that in Nicaragua 'he grew outrageously passionate, in so much that he drew his cutlass, slashed open the heart of a poor Spaniard, and pulling it out began to gnaw it, saying to the rest, "I will serve you all alike if you don't talk." ' Other tortures included, 'besides burning with matches and suchlike slight torments, to cut a man to pieces, first some flesh, then a hand, an arm, a leg, sometimes tying a cord about his head and with a stick twisting it till his eyes shoot out, which is called woolding.'

We are told that Lolonois had an appropriately awful end, being captured by Darien Indians who 'tore him to pieces, throwing his body limb by limb into the fire'. His death did not deter other buccaneers from following his example. Leaders like Morgan and Grammont may not have shared Lolonois' psychopathic extremism, but they could not prevent their men from using very similar methods of extortion. For these mercenary gangs, living off the land and anxious to get away before the Spaniards could launch a counter-

François Lolonois, by all accounts the most bloodthirsty of the big-time buccaneers, who in the 1660s took to systematic land-raiding.

attack, terror was taken for granted and had to be administered in ever larger doses as the 'enemy' grew accustomed to it. During the six years of Morgan's ascendancy (1665–71) the buccaneers, still recruited on an international basis, sacked eighteen cities, four towns, and nearly forty villages: Cumaná once, Cumanagote twice, Maracaibo and Gibraltar twice, Rio de la Hacha five times, Santa Marta three times, Tolú eight times, Portobello once, Chagre twice, Panama once, Santa Catalina twice, Granada de Nicaragua twice, Campeche three times, Santiago de Cuba once, and other towns and villages in Cuba and Hispaniola up to 120 miles inland so often that no accurate count is possible. This estimate does not include English ravages in later years, or the still more indiscriminate French onslaughts. Seldom have a few thousand mercenary desperadoes exercised a reign of terror over so vast a region. Alarmed lest the international buccaneer groups – Mansfield's companies, for instance, included Frenchmen, Hollanders, Portuguese, Greeks,

Henry Morgan, a ruthless exponent of pirate imperialism, who was knighted for his services and appointed Deputy Governor of Jamaica.

Amerindians and Negroes – should cut loose from any pretence of control, the French, English and Dutch Governors were mainly concerned to keep them in some kind of semi-official employment.

Henry Morgan, though a leader of considerable ability, owes his fame to his perch on the shoulders of the Old Guard. The difference was that he happened to be a comparatively civilized outsider who mustered even larger armadas than those of Lolonois (about two thousand buccaneers for the attack on Panama), was knighted by Charles II for his anti-Spanish exploits, settled in Jamaica as a wealthy planter (and Deputy Governor and Justice of the Peace), and, like his French equivalent Laurens de Graaf, eventually sat in judgment on his former associates in a classic poacher-turned-gamekeeper switch.

Though the evidence is not conclusive, it is generally accepted that Morgan was born in 1635 at Llanrhymney, Glamorganshire, the eldest son of Robert Morgan. He was later to sue Exquemelin's English publishers for describing him as a monster of cruelty, but more particularly for describing his father as a yeoman farmer. He insisted that he was 'a gentleman's son', and vigorously denied that he had been transported to Barbados – though he did not reveal why or when he arrived in the West Indies or what he was doing in the years before 1665. One theory is that he came to Jamaica with Cromwell's army in 1655. It is certain that he had useful connections with the embryo colonial establishment in Jamaica. His uncle, Sir Edward Morgan, was in 1663 appointed Deputy Governor to Sir Thomas Modyford, a wealthy Barbados planter – and the man who provided commissions and excuses (notably a Spanish invasion scare) for the buccaneers.

A few episodes stand out from the wearisome butchery of the Morgan era. In 1665 a detachment of buccaneers defended the island of Santa Catalina off the coast of Costa Rica by using 'batteries of sixty muskets fastened together like organ pipes and firing simultaneously'. During his siege of Portobello, Morgan forced a batch of captured priests and nuns up scaling ladders as shields for buccaneer bombers: a sacrilegious set-piece that angered Exquemelin, who, like other flibustiers, remained a Catholic at heart and a stern critic of *corsarios luteranos* who never knew where to draw the line. In 1669, while he was preparing for another raid on Maracaibo, Morgan's flagship, the *Oxford*, blew up in the harbour of Port Royal during a riotous council of war, killing over two hundred men, five captains among them. Only Morgan and about twenty-five officers sitting on his side of the table survived. The sea was full of corpses, and buccaneers from other ships rowed out to salvage boots, swords and pistols, hacking off fingers if there were rings of any value on them. The explosion was probably caused by the carelessness of a drunken gunner, but Morgan blamed it on the treachery of the French buccaneers.

This disaster temporarily shook his prestige, but a year later he was gathering another and much bigger fleet for the Panama expedition. Despite the bad feeling caused by the *Oxford* incident there were five hundred Frenchmen in a force of nearly two thousand marauders. The thirty-six ships were still small and tightly packed, ranging from a flagship of 120 tons and twenty-two guns to an unarmed sloop of twelve tons (by 1684 flibustier admirals like Grammont and de Graaf used larger vessels with over fifty guns and three hundred men, but their squadrons still contained two-gun midgets with crews of twenty). Preparations for the campaign went on throughout the autumn of 1670. Victualling was the main problem. Raids on Spanish hog-yards and cattle-ranches were carried out on a large scale, and a squadron cruised along the coast of the Main seizing cargoes of foodstuffs and extracting a ransom of four thousand bushels of grain from Rio de la Hacha.

The expedition was approved by a unanimous vote of the Jamaica

Morgan's men sacking Puerto del Principe, Cuba. The disadvantage of large-scale raid was that the booty had to be vas to satisfy everyone involved, an as time went on the law of diminishing returns began to operate.

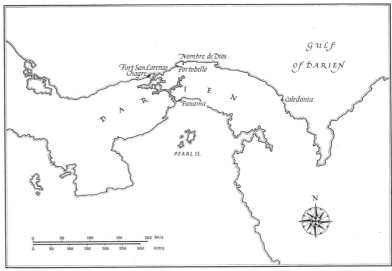

The Isthmus of Darien, as Panama was known at the time of the buccaneers.

Council on what Modyford called 'the old, pleasing account of no purchase, no pay'. The articles stipulated that the spoil was to be divided into equal shares, of which each captain drew a certain number, allocated according to rank. Compensation for injuries was – on paper – higher than usual, since ambitious land campaigns involved a much greater risk of mortality and serious wounds. Six hundred Spanish dollars were to be paid for the loss of a hand or a leg; 1800 dollars for both hands; 1500 for both legs; for an eye, a hundred dollars – or the equivalent in slaves could be taken at a valuation of a hundred dollars per slave. The first man to enter a fort under fire or to haul down the Spanish colours was to get a reward of fifty dollars. After these sums had been paid out, the seamen were to share what remained. Each company signed the articles, about two-thirds writing their names – a much higher proportion than in the early days: buccaneering was beginning to attract a different class of adventurer.

Sailing in December 1670 in feigned ignorance of the fact that a treaty just signed in Madrid had recognized British territorial claims in the West Indies, Morgan paused at Providence Island en route to Fort San Lorenzo at the mouth of the river Chagre. Overawed by the size of the fleet, the Governor agreed to surrender on condition that Morgan staged a mock assault, using powder but no shot, and that the garrison should be taken to the mainland and released. After this sham victory, the storming of San Lorenzo, with its garrison of 350 well-armed troops, proved a bloody business, during which at least a hundred buccaneers were killed and seventy severely wounded. Leaving three hundred men to occupy the fort and 150 to guard the fleet, Morgan, with 1,400 buccaneers in a flotilla of sloops and *piraguas*, set out early in January 1671 on the fifty-mile journey to Panama.

Sandbars forced the men to march along the river banks to lighten the boats. Swampy ground and dense jungle slowed their progress. The larger sloops had to be abandoned, and another two hundred men left behind to protect them. Food was hard to come by, and after four days the buccaneers were glad to make a meal of leather bags softened in water, beaten between stones to make them less tough, then cut into strips and roasted. By the sixth day they were physical wrecks, taking turns to march or paddle. At any time they could have been routed by determined ambushers. But the Spanish forces retreated, hoping to give them the *coup de grâce* on the open plain around the city of Panama. On the seventh day, the buccaneers ate every stray cat and dog they found in the burned-out village of Venta de Cruz.

Wine, women, song and loot for Henry Morgan: a nineteenth-century French illustrator's version of the pirate dream.

On the eighth day they survived a hail of arrows from Indians while passing through a narrow defile. On the ninth day they struggled up to resume the march at dawn. Around noon they came in sight of the South Sea and of a wide plain teeming with cattle. 'At once', wrote Exquemelin, 'the men broke ranks and shot down every beast within range. While some hunted others lit fires to roast the meat – bulls, cows, horses, mules. The animals were hacked up and the pieces thrown on the fire. . . . The meat scarcely had time to get hot before they grabbed it and began gnawing, gore running down their cheeks and beards.'

The Spanish force was much larger than that of Morgan, but it was poorly armed and the infantry, largely composed of Indian and Negro slaves, was no match for the deadly musketeers. A cavalry charge across a swamp was broken up by the fire of an advance guard of two hundred crack French skirmishers. 'Each man went down on one knee and they fired by turns – one man aiming while his neighbour reloaded, so their fusillade never paused.' A herd of cattle, stampeded from the rear with the idea of trampling and scattering the pirates, hurtled on through opened ranks to complete the confusion of the defenders. In the street fighting that followed, Panama went up in flames. Two large galleons crammed with treasure (including, it was said, a magnificent gold altarpiece) had sailed south, and mule-trains laden with valuables had vanished into the highlands towards Mexico.

As had been the case with other large-scale expeditions, the booty was disappointingly, even derisively, small when divided among so many. On Morgan's orders, ships captured in harbour were dismasted to prevent disgruntled companies from starting a South Sea plunder cruise on their own account. Morgan was accused of cheating when the final share-out was made at Chagre late in February, though he made a great show of allowing himself and his baggage to be publicly searched – and infuriated French buccaneer captains by forcing them to do likewise. Backed by Modyford, the Jamaican militia, and a bodyguard of ruthless thugs, Morgan was able to ignore complaints. Richard Browne, surgeon-general to the

*William Dampier
1651–1715), Pirate and
Hydrographer' : the only
buccaneer to have his portrait
painted.*

buccaneer fleet, reported that 'the commanders dared but seldom appear' and that 'the widows, orphans and injured inhabitants who had so freely advanced upon the hopes of a glorious design, were now ruined'.

Morgan died in 1688, three years after the arrival of a naval squadron in Port Royal obliged him to curtail his continued undercover dabbling in buccaneer ventures. No doubt, as Burney remarked, he was a great rogue; but he and Modyford could plead that their activities as the duumvirs of buccaneer imperialism had forced the Spaniards to come to terms with reality and made sure that the terms of the Treaty of Madrid would be observed. Though he showed little imagination and was essentially a land commander, Morgan has been celebrated in ballads as the greatest of the buccaneers. Sometimes he is a bogeyman:

Him cheat him friend of him last guinea
Him kill both friar and priest – O dear!
Him cut de t'roat of piccaninny,
Bloody, bloody buccaneer!

Sometimes there is a note of nostalgia:

You was a flyer, Morgan,
You was the lad to crowd,
When you was in your flagship,
But now you're in your shroud.

After the sack of Panama, Port Royal was officially closed as a buccaneer base. Tortuga survived as such for another thirty years, with Grammont, de Graaf, van Horn and the Marquis de Maintenon let loose to put on the pressure until the Spaniards recognized French claims to 'the riches of the Indies'. Like Morgan, these leaders were poles apart from the wild, improvident roughnecks of the Old Guard. Nobly-born outsiders like Maintenon and Ravenau de Lussan came to the Caribbean to repair shattered fortunes, cashing in on the weakness of a Spanish empire groggy from a corsair gruelling that had lasted for a century and a half. Grammont established himself for six months at a base near Maracaibo, whence he systematically ravaged the coast of New Granada. Vera Cruz was sacked while the Spanish fleet, outnumbered and outgunned, stood off and on outside the harbour until the buccaneers – many of them English or Dutch – were ready to leave.

The last real spark of buccaneer daring was struck when smaller, independent Anglo-French expeditions began to cross the Darien Isthmus in 1679. 'That which often spurs men on to the undertaking of the most difficult adventure', wrote one corsair, 'is the sacred hunger of gold . . . 'twas gold was the bait that tempted a pack of merry boys of us, near 300, being all soldiers of fortune'; and he added, with a characteristic, if fantastic, clutch at legality, that he and his mates had enlisted 'in the service of one of the richest West Indian monarchs, the [Indian] Emperor of Darien'. In 1685 these roving companies came very close to capturing Panama and, but for dissensions between the various contingents, each sporting its own banner, might well have established a pirate republic on the Pacific coast of the Isthmus. This was the era chronicled by William Dampier, Lionel Wafer and Basil Ringrose, representatives, like Ravenaù de Lussan, of a new sprinkling of highly literate freebooters as greedy for knowledge and experience as for gold. Through all the vicissitudes of a pirate marathon that took him round the world in twelve years and as many different ships, Dampier, the son of a farmer at East Coker in Somerset, carefully preserved his charts and journals rolled up in lengths of bamboo sealed with wax. Ringrose, a runaway apprentice, had a smattering of Latin which was useful for interrogating Spanish priests.

The Chevalier de Grammont, one of several impoverished French nobles who sought to repair their fortunes as buccaneer captains in the 1680s

The Galapagos Islands (rich with turtles) in the north, and the island of Juan Fernandez off the coast of Chile, became the two main bases for a series of strikes along and upon the South Sea coast. Captaincies often changed hands, and a number of persistent mutineers were put ashore – sometimes voluntarily, since it was easy enough to hollow out a *piragua*, grab a Spanish prize, and start up in business again. Plans and destinations were changed so frequently – some companies made for the East Indies, others for the Gulf of Guinea – that the buccaneer eruption into the South Sea (which Morgan had vetoed in 1671) developed into an almost inextricable muddle. Bartholomew Sharp's cruise alone has a certain cohesion and continuity. Twice deposed from the captaincy, but re-elected as the most skilled 'sea artist' (expert in navigation), he met with very mixed fortunes. The biggest treasure haul – four hundred ingots of rough silver taken in the *Santa Rosario* – was mistaken for tin and heaved overboard. According to a member of the crew who kept one ingot and brought it back to England, Sharp was more interested in 620 jars of brandy and a woman passenger described by Ringrose as 'the most beautiful I ever saw in all the South Sea'.

When, having rounded Cape Horn from the Pacific in a howling storm (a pioneer feat), Sharp sailed into the Caribbean in January 1682 after a two-year absence, he got a cool reception from some of the more zealously anti-piratical authorities. Chased from Barbados by a naval frigate and refused permission to land by the Governor of Antigua, he finally got ashore at Nevis. From there he and Ringrose got a passage to England, taking with them some plunder from the *Santa Rosario* whose value Sharp had not been too intoxicated or infatuated to recognize. 'In this prize', he exulted in his journal, 'I took a Spanish manuscript of a prodigious value – it describes all the ports, roads, harbours, bays, sands, rocks and rising of the land, and instructions how to work a ship into any port or harbour. They were going to throw it overboard but by good luck I saved it. The

Spaniards cried out when I got the book (farewell South Seas now).'

In London, 'for want of evidence' (actually because he presented
Charles II with a superbly embellished copy of the charts stolen from
the *Santa Rosario*), Sharp was not only acquitted of piracy but given
command of a sloop-of-war and commissioned to 'apprehend
Indians and pirates' in the Caribbean. Surviving two further trials
for piracy – his partner in plunder, the Governor of Nevis, swore that
'the evidence of a crew of dogs should not take away the life of an
Englishman' – he was last heard of in 1688 as 'Governor' of Snake
Island (Anguilla), presiding over a population described as 'without
government or religion', selling dubious commissions freely to old
friends, and lighting his pipe with summonses for his arrest.

When in 1674, at the end of a comfortable two-year 'detention' in
London for the 'crime of Panama', Morgan was knighted by Charles
II and received his instructions as Lieutenant-Governor of Jamaica
from the philosopher John Locke (then Clerk to the Board of Trade),
he proved that a buccaneer of prowess was not likely to be without
honour in his native land. Sharp's charts had made him the toast of
the Admiralty, and in 1691 Dampier brought back with him (as his
fellow stowaway on an East Indiaman) an elaborately tattooed Malay
boy out of whom he planned to make money as an exotic freak. The
unfortunate Painted Prince was soon sold to a showman, and died of
smallpox after a few months of relentless exploitation; but in the
meantime he had served to give Dampier an entrée into fashionable
society.

Dampier's journals, published in four volumes between 1697

*West Indian traders bartering
and stowing their gains. By the
start of the eighteenth century
the increasing volume of French
English and Dutch colonial
trade offered alternative prizes
for pirates, some of them
Spanish.*

and 1709 as *A New Voyage Round the World*, quickly rivalled
Exquemelin's book as a best-seller, and he was fêted by Samuel
Pepys, John Evelyn, and members of the newly formed Royal
Society. Sir Hans Sloane, who succeeded Isaac Newton as the
Society's President in 1727, collected the journals of Dampier,
Wafer, Sharp and Ringrose as compilations of scientific and historical interest: and they were among the first items to be deposited in the
library of the British Museum, for the foundation of which Sloane
was chiefly responsible. A century later Burney wrote of Dampier's
narratives that 'it is not easy to name another voyager who has given
more useful information to the world; to whom the merchant and
mariner are so much indebted; or who has communicated his
information in a more unembarrassed or intelligible manner'. They
certainly influenced Defoe, both in style and subject-matter: and
Dampier was the only buccaneer to have his portrait painted. The
picture is now in the National Portrait Gallery and its caption –
'Pirate and Hydrographer' – shows a nice sense of balance.

In one of his more arresting and recherché passages (about Sal, an
island in the Bay of Honduras) Dampier writes that 'when many
flamingoes stand together at a distance they appear like a brick wall;
for their feathers are of the colour of new red brick, and except when
feeding they commonly stand upright exactly in a row close by each
other'. He adds that 'a dish of flamingoes' tongues is fit for a prince's
table; they are large and have a knob of fat at the root which is an
excellent bit'.

Lionel Wafer, the buccaneer surgeon, had even more exotic tales to tell in his *New Voyage and Description of the Isthmus of Panama* (1699) when he arrived in London after an odyssey as far-flung as Dampier's. With two comrades, Edward Davis and John Hingson, he had spent two years in jail at Jamestown, Virginia. At the end of five years' pirating in the Atlantic, the Caribbean and the South Sea, his personal booty was listed by the authorities as 'in one bag, 37 silver plates; two scollops; seven dishes, silver lace, seven cups broken . . . three bags of Spanish money containing 1,100 dollars . . . in a chest marked LW a piece of cloth and some old things, with old broken plate and some little basins'. In 1691, after interminable litigation, the three men (who insisted that they were West Indian merchants who had traded with privateers) were released. Three hundred pounds' worth of their loot was set aside 'to be applied to the building of a college or to such other charitable object as the King shall direct'. It probably went towards the construction of William and Mary College at Williamsburg.

Steering clear of this and other less edifying episodes, Wafer's book concentrates on an account of his sojourn among the Cuna Indians of Darien in 1681. The Cunans were greatly impressed by his blood-letting technique, which proved more efficient and less painful than the method they had been accustomed to use. In this, the patient was stripped naked, seated on a stone in the middle of a stream, and peppered with miniature arrows shot into the flesh to a depth of about half an inch. 'If by chance they hit a vein and the blood spurts out a little', wrote Wafer, 'the medicine men will leap and skip about, showing many antick gestures by way of rejoicing and triumph.' Wafer's lancet gave him a privileged status, and he was obliged to go completely native. Painted from head to foot in vivid vegetable dyes, he wore a lip-plate of hammered gold and a silver penis-holder shaped like a cone and supported by a thong round the waist, and took part in heroic drinking bouts when the effects of huge quantities of palm liquor and corn beer were slept off in hammocks while women sponged the men's overheated bodies to keep them cool. He reported that the Cuna language reminded him of Gaelic, noted down a basic vocabulary which proved helpful to anthropologists two centuries later, and gave an idyllic account of the gentleness of the Cunans, the perfection of the climate, and the abundance of fruits, wild pig and deer.

Dampier and Wafer were much sought after as consultants by English merchants and financiers about to form a South Sea Company, and in 1696 were formally interviewed by a Committee of Enquiry, one of whose members was John Locke. But the promoters of the ill-fated Scottish Darien Company closed in on Wafer and hauled him off to Edinburgh convinced that they were going to steal a march on the Sassenachs. Their tight-fistedness may have inspired Wafer to flights of vengefully misleading rhetoric in which the coastline of the Gulf of Darien was represented as an earthly paradise. Certainly his book and his verbal elaborations upon it were

The Cuna Indian method of blood-letting, as described by Lionel Wafer in his journal.

decisive factors in the greedily wishful thinking that resulted in the catastrophic fiasco of the colony of Caledonia. Plagued by malaria, jungle sores, and fierce tropical storms, and attacked as pirates by the Spaniards, more than a thousand Scottish emigrants perished in Wafer's alleged paradise before it was ignominiously abandoned.

Dampier, whose travelogues provided Jonathan Swift with much material for *Gulliver's Travels*, sailed as commander of the *Roebuck* on a voyage of exploration to Australia in 1699. It was not a success (Dampier was cashiered). Nor was his privateering cruise of 1702–4 in the Pacific. Drinking heavily, Dampier proved a capricious and irresolute captain, and failed dismally in an attempt to capture a Manila galleon. Bickering was so incessant that Alexander Selkirk, quartermaster of the *Cinque Ports*, asked to be put ashore on Juan Fernandez. Four years later, when Dampier revisited the island on another and far more disciplined and successful privateering cruise (1708–11) as pilot to Captain Woodes Rogers in the *Duke*, Selkirk – 'a man clothed in goat skins who looked wilder than their first owners' – was rescued: and Woodes Rogers's account of his epic of survival gave Defoe the idea for *Robinson Crusoe*.

Chapter Five **Black Jack and Blackbeard**

The Rev. Cotton Mather (1663–1728), a Boston divine famed for his unctuous gallows-foot sermons to pirates and other malefactors.

When the buccaneers had completed their job of sapping Spanish power they became a political, economic and social embarrassment. The bribes they offered to their friends on the Jamaica Council, or to French, Dutch and Danish Governors, were still sometimes accepted. But citizens of substance, who had developed their plantations behind a pirate shield, now longed to be rid of their wayward protectors.

Buccaneering, they argued, had stripped Jamaica of able-bodied men and retarded the development of its natural resources. Between 1668 and 1671 alone, complained one report, over 2,500 men had gone on the account: a very large number in a weak colony surrounded by enemies. 'People have not married, built or settled. . . Privateering encourages all manner of disorder and dissoluteness and if it succeed, does but enrich the worst sort of people and provoke and alarm the Spaniards. . . . The number of tippling houses is now doubly increased, so that there is not now resident ten men to every house that selleth strong liquors. There are more than a hundred licensed houses, besides sugar and rum works that sell without licence.'

But giving the bum's rush to these undesirable allies was not so easy. Few buccaneers were tempted by the offer of plots of indifferent land or by the prospect of working for rich employers who looked askance on them. They accepted pardons when it suited them, but 'black' ships continued to appear off remote beaches to take on crews and there was never any lack of recruits. The naval squadron that arrived in Port Royal in 1685 did not chalk up many successes. In 1687 Captain Spragge came in with four pirates – as they had now become in the vocabulary of the Jamaican bourgeoisie – hanging at the yard-arm. But juries still acquitted them on technicalities, and the more disreputable members of the colonial Old Guard on the Council, including Morgan, fought a long delaying action, reasoning that it would be unwise to force a total buccaneer exodus which would leave Jamaica without adequate naval defence, strengthen the hand of French and Dutch rivals, and benefit the economy of other, mostly foreign, islands.

It seemed that the prayers of their opponents had been spectacularly answered when on 7 June 1692 Port Royal, often known as 'the wickedest city in Christendom', was devastated by an earthquake. God Himself seemed to have spoken out for economic sanity and moral progress. Eye-witnesses described how, after a morning of intolerable heat and sinister silence (no birdsong or insect noises), the island was shaken by three shocks of increasing severity accompanied by roars of thunder. The sea, until that moment uncannily smooth, reared up in a series of tidal waves. The tremors continued for three weeks and Port Royal, built along a sandspit, was almost entirely obliterated. Ships were torn from anchorage and swept inland over the sunken ruins. Few houses were left standing, and nearly two thousand people had been drowned or entombed as the earth split.

Port Royal was sunk beyond recall; but many English buccaneers joined the flibustiers, and from 1680 onwards pirates of all nationalities had found a warm welcome not only in peripheral West Indian islands but in the ports of New England. In New York City, councillor-businessmen sold them gunpowder and provisions at a fat profit. Boston authorities found it convenient to accept the story that French and English 'plate ships' had acquired their cargoes by salvaging wrecks in the Florida Channel. When Bostonians, fearing that their city might become a second Port Royal, began to make difficulties, the Governor of Rhode Island proved more obliging. Pardons were freely sold and blatantly forged commissions barely scrutinized. When, in 1699, the American colonies were empowered to set up their own Admiralty Courts – before that pirates had to be sent back to England to stand trial – the law was easily bent to the needs of the new patrons of free enterprise on the high seas. George Larkin, sent from England to appoint Commissioners for Piracy, got little co-operation and reported that pirates were 'entertained and caressed, even by the Church people'. During a visit to Bermuda he was clapped into jail by Governor Bennett on a trumped-up charge of raping a Negro woman, and died soon after his release.

The recall of Nicholas Trott, Governor of the Bahamas, for taking large bribes from pirates, was considered very unfair by men like Bennett – who had exchanged a shipload of French prisoners-of-war for a cargo of liquor instead of English captives. Colonial officials were grossly underpaid, and in America had no such opportunities for advancement at the expense of the natives as had the officers of the East India Company. A rake-off from piracy and smuggling was their main source of supplementary income.

Even when a pirate broke the rules too flagrantly and had to be made an example of, as happened at Boston in 1704 to John Quelch (who had plundered Portuguese instead of French shipping), most of the booty stayed with his judges. 'Oh,' apostrophized the Rev. Cotton Mather, who was well paid for his sermon, 'that the poor men which are immediately to appear before the awful Tribunal of God may first by Sovereign Grace have produced upon their Souls those Marks of Thy Favour. . . . Oh, Great God, let thy Sovereign Grace operate on this fearful occasion!' Quelch, unmoved by this, 'pulled off his hat, bowed to the spectators, and replied: "Gentlemen! 'tis but little I have to say to my fellows, save this. Take care how you bring Money into New England, to be hanged for it.'''

Quelch, who had been elected leader after the crew of the privateer *Charles* had mutinied and killed their captain, seems to have been one of the first pirates to fly the Jolly Roger, or black jack. (Privateers sailed under their national flag or the flag of the commissioning country. Sometimes, when summoning a ship to surrender, they ran up a red flag, meaning that no quarter would be granted if there was any resistance.) The earliest record of a Jolly Roger occurs in 1700, when a French pirate flew 'a sable ensign with cross-bones, a death's head and an hour-glass' during an engagement with an English man-of-war off Jamaica. The hour-glass may have been a hint that there was not much time for deliberation, a point reinforced by the skull-and-bones, a traditional symbol of death.

The devices on the jack varied. Quelch's showed 'an anatomy with an hour-glass in one hand and in the other a dart in a heart with three drops of blood proceeding from it'. Other crews favoured a black pennant with a skeleton holding a glass of rum punch in one hand and a cutlass in the other, or put a black or red skeleton on a white ground.

Reports indicate that the Roger was run up first, to signify an offer of quarter, and the bloody flag flown if the offer was rejected. In *An Account of his Capture by Captain Spriggs and his Sufferings Amongst the Pirates of the Spanish Main in the Year 1724*, Captain Richard Hawkins wrote: 'About eleven o'clock one night, after the whole crew had been some time assembled in the great cabin, I heard three huzzas and then they all came up on deck and hoisted *Jolly Roger* (for so they called their black ensign, in the middle of which is a large white skeleton with a dart in one hand striking a bleeding heart, and in the other an hour-glass). . . . When they fight under *Jolly Roger* they give quarter, which they do not when they fight under the red or bloody flag.'

Three main theories about the origin of the term 'Jolly Roger' have been put forward: that the flibustiers called the red flag the *joli rouge*, that this was easily corrupted to jolly roger by English buccaneers, and that the name was later applied to the black flag; that Ali Raja, a Tamil pirate captain, flew a red flag and English pirates in the Indian Ocean began to call it Ally Roger, Olly Roger, Old Roger, then Jolly Roger; and that the term derived from the English 'roger' meaning a vagabond rogue. A more plausible explanation is that the black jack was a 'godless' challenge to a hypocritical Cotton Mather-type society. In 1725 the *New Canting Dictionary* listed Old Roger as a synonym for the Devil, and there was surely a certain cynical defiance in the pirates' symbolism. Whatever the truth of this matter, the black jack represented an attempt to revive the anarchic, comradely spirit of the Old Guard buccaneers and to create a kind of occupational *esprit de corps*.

The long French war of Queen Anne's reign kept most pirates busy privateering, but in 1713, as it drew to a close, there were signs

n America, as in England, any
terature connected with piracy
as certain to have a wide
opular appeal.

THE
TRIALS

Of Eight Perſons

Indited for Piracy &c.

Of whom Two were acquitted,
and the reſt found Guilty.

At a Juſticiary Court of Admiralty Aſſembled and Held in Boſton within His Majeſty's Province of the Maſſachuſetts-Bay in New-England, on the 18th of **October** 1717. and by ſeveral Adjournments continued to the 30th. Purſuant to His Majeſty's Commiſſion and Inſtructions, founded on the Act of Parliament Made in the 11th. & 12th of KING William IIId. Intituled, *An Act for the more effectual Suppreſſion of Piracy.*

With an APPENDIX,

Containing the Subſtance of their Confeſſions given before His Excellency the Governour, when they were firſt brought to *Boſton*, and committed to Goal.

Boſton :

Printed by **B. Green**, for **John Edwards**, and Sold at his Shop in King's Street. 1718.

of a chaotic aftermath. A Jamaican planter forecast that twelve years of licensed plunder would 'leave to the world a brood of pirates' and that expanding British colonial trade was likely to get the kind of treatment hitherto reserved for the Spaniards. In 1714 *guarda-costas*, whose crews also worked on a no-purchase-no-pay basis, began to snatch prizes in Jamaican harbours, while the few naval frigates available were escorting merchantmen into the Atlantic. Puerto Rico was 'a nest of pirates . . . who under the pretence of being *guarda-costas* plague the American Seas'. The Bahamas were used as a base by such characters as Augustino Blanco, a Spanish outlaw presiding over a shifting population of Spanish, Portuguese, English, Scottish, mulatto and Negro pirates. Nassau, the principal town of New Providence, had been destroyed in 1703 by a Franco-Spanish expedition. Since then it had been without a government and almost without inhabitants, most of whom had fled to the Carolinas. The Lords Proprietors seemed to have lost interest in the island, and ex-privateers moved in to inaugurate a short-lived pirate republic. In July 1716 Governor Spotswood of Virginia sent news of this development to London: 'A nest of pirates are endeavouring to establish themselves in New Providence, and by the additions they expect and will probably receive by loosely disordered people from the Bay of Campeachy, Jamaica and other parts may prove dangerous to British commerce if not timely suppressed.' By this time the pirate republic had a population of about two thousand outlaws, led by Henry Jennings, Charles Vane, Charles Bellamy, Oliver la Bouche, Benjamin Hornigold, and Hornigold's lieutenant, Edward Teach. With five ships and three hundred men, Jennings and Vane had caused a diplomatic crisis by seizing 350,000 pieces of eight from a Spanish salvage crew who had spent months raising treasure from the wrecks of a plate fleet sunk by a hurricane off the Bahamas.

Nassau was a shanty town of driftwood and palm fronds and old sails draped over spars to make tents. It was said that when the wind blew from the land you could smell New Providence before you sighted it. Every other hovel was a grog shop or a brothel with Negro and mulatto prostitutes. Favourite drinks were rumfustian (a mixture of beer, gin and sherry, heavily spiced) and rum and gunpowder, and according to Defoe 'sobriety brought a man under suspicion'. A sail-maker's widow sewed black jacks to order in return for a generous ration of brandy, and the general atmosphere resembled that of Hogarth's Gin Lane in a balmy climate, or of a resurrected and even sleazier Port Royal.

Yet it was not all booze, sloth, brawl and guffaw. Like the pirate 'democracies' of ancient Greece, this loose association of independent companies or 'commonwealths' functioned efficiently and with surprisingly little friction. Without the benefit of political theory, this tough collection of turned-off naval auxiliaries hit on a way of life that was close to anarchism; and it worked, as anarchism on a small scale often does if left to itself. There were few written

Major Stede Bonnet, hanged at
Charleston in 1718, when the
American Admiralty Courts
had become more effective.

laws, but by common consent the defence of the commonwealth was
undertaken by such companies as happened to be in port. A battery
was raised and manned in rotation by a garrison of fifty men.
Working clothes consisted of jerkins and short, loose trousers of
sailcloth thickly smeared with pitch: a kind of light armour capable of
turning aside dagger thrusts and cutlass swipes. Ships' articles,
following privateer precedent but modified by a profound mistrust of
authority, were drawn up by a 'learned' pirate (such as Major Stede
Bonnet, a Barbados planter who went on the account, some said to
escape his wife's shrewish temper), read out and signed. The
following do's and don'ts were typical of most companies:

1 Every man shall obey civil command; the captain shall have one full share and a half in all prizes; the master, carpenter, boatswain and gunner [known as 'artists'] shall have one share and a quarter.

2 If any man shall offer to run away or keep any secret from the company, he shall be marooned with one bottle of powder, one bottle of water, one small arm and shot.

3 If any man shall steal anything in the company, or game, to the value of a piece of eight, he shall be marroon'd or shot.

4 If at any time we should meet another Marrooner [pirate ship], that man that shall sign his articles without the consent of our company shall suffer such punishment as the captain and company shall think fit.

5 That man that shall strike another whilst these articles are in force shall receive Moses' Law (that is 40 stripes lacking one) on the bare back.

6 That man that shall snap his arms, or smoke tobacco in the hold without a cap to his pipe, or carry a candle lighted without a lanthorn, shall suffer the same punishment as in the former article.

7 That man that shall not keep his arms clean, fit for an engagement, or neglect his business, shall be cut off from his share and suffer such other punishment as the captain and the company shall think fit.

8 If any man shall lose a joint in time of an engagement he shall have 400 pieces of eight; if a limb 800.

9 If at any time you meet with a prudent woman, that man that offers to meddle with her without her consent shall suffer present death.

Women on board, like gambling for high stakes, were known to cause strife and indiscipline. Because of the growing power of the Bahaman pirates and their not undeserved reputation as sex maniacs, few women travelled by sea in the Caribbean except on a naval ship. If female prisoners were taken, they were guarded by the company's champion bruiser; if he did not always resist temptation – and some women offered themselves to their warder on the principle that this was the surest way of avoiding multiple rape – he usually kept the rest of the crew at bay. John ('Calico Jack') Rackham, Vane's former quartermaster who formed his own company after being voted out for cowardice, seems to have been the only leader to relax the stag rule, and allow two women – Anne Bonny and Mary Read – on board. Defoe spins a long, highly improbable story to the effect that Anne remained faithful to Calico Jack and Mary gave herself to no one but her chosen lover. He also states that both managed to conceal

Anne Bonny and Mary Read, the only known exceptions to the strict pirate rule not to allow 'trouble-making' women on board.

their sex from the rest of the crew until brought to trial in Jamaica in 1720, when they startled the judge by announcing that they were pregnant ('My Lord, we plead our bellies').

The most likely explanation for these so-called female pirates is that they were taken on as whores, being, as several witnesses remarked during the trial, 'not detained by force but very active and willing to do anything'. Even so, their presence led to jealousy and brawls. Two French 'artists' who had been forced to join Rackham's company asserted that 'when we gave chase or attacked they wore men's clothes; at all other times they wore women's clothes'. This suggests that the women put on trousers and jerkins for physical convenience and made no attempt at sustained impersonation. Some theorists maintain that if they had done so the affairs with Rackham and Mary's anonymous lover might have been passed off as homosexual liaisons. This seems unlikely. Large naval vessels by this time provided wooden latrines rigged in a secluded part of the deck; but on sloops of fifty tons or so such as the pirates still used there was no such refinement. The crew had to urinate and excrete squatting in 'the head' – the forechains of the bow. One has to assume that they were not crassly unobservant and that they would immediately have invoked the basic pirate principle of fair shares. The captain, whose privileges were so closely circumscribed, would have been the last person to be allowed a private concubine – or catamite. But Defoe's version was a pretty peg for bourgeois fantasy, and Anne Bonny and Mary Read were among the few pirates to be given a ballad to themselves:

With pitch and tar their hands were hard
Tho' once like velvet soft,
They weigh'd the anchor, heav'd the lead,
And boldly went aloft . . .

Their disruptive effect on discipline convinced the pirates once and for all of the dangers of laxity. What had hitherto been an unwritten rule was now often clearly stated in a separate clause. In some cases the ban extended to young boys too, as in the articles of Bartholomew Roberts: 'No boy or woman to be allowed amongst the company. If any man is found lying with any of the latter sex or carries a woman to sea disguised, he is to suffer Death.'

New Providence offered splendid natural facilities – fresh spring water, fruit, turtles, pigs and cattle, and a superb natural harbour capable of accommodating up to five hundred sloops, barques and brigantines, but approached by two narrow entrances too shallow to be negotiated by ships-of-the-line. Ships could be careened in safety and were overhauled every three or four weeks. The general aim was a quick turnover, with many but small prizes (the Caribbean equivalent of the tactics of the English rovers of the fifteenth and sixteenth centuries). Captured vessels of suitable size were 'cut down', all superfluous structures being removed to make the decks flush and unencumbered. If they were too large, they were often burned and the crews and passengers put ashore. Chases sometimes ended by 'clapping aboard' with grapnels and boarding-nets to a blare of trumpets and a rattle of drums, for close-quarter fighting with pistols and cutlasses, grenades and smoky, smelly, confusion-enhancing stinkpots. But a show of force and a hoisting of the Roger was often enough, especially as naval commanders in the West Indies had what amounted to a vested interest in piracy.

he Jolly Roger as flown by
:alico Jack' Rackham, and
(ight) a pennant stiffened with
ttens.

Men-of-war were hired out for convoy duty at stiff rates (up to $12\frac{1}{2}$ per cent of a cargo's value) – a much more profitable business than chasing robbers. The money was easily earned, since pirates rarely attacked an escorted convoy. But if piracy were suppressed there would be no need for escorts: so an unwritten non-aggression pact was observed on both sides. Naval ships often carried freight – illegally, but since they offered lower rates and higher security their services were in great demand. The result, as the Governor of Jamaica complained, was a slump in merchant shipping and a mob of out-of-work seamen who were likely to turn pirate. At the same time, Spanish raids on the logwood camps around the Bay of Campeche, which for some time had provided an alternative to sea robbery, forced several hundred more men to go on the account.

This was not the most profitable era of piracy, but it was probably the least hazardous. The chief danger was that there would not be enough prizes to go round, even on a modest scale. By 1718, trade in the West Indies was almost paralysed. 'I do not think it advisable to go from here except upon an extraordinary occasion, not knowing but that I may be intercepted by pirates,' wrote the Governor of the

Leeward Islands. This overkill forced many pirates to step up their activities off the North American coast, and to cash in on their contacts with sympathetic officials – particularly in North Carolina which, unlike South Carolina and Virginia, was a poor colony without a flourishing export trade. The pirates could undercut regular smugglers (who had been buying up their stolen goods at New Providence), and, having dispensed with middlemen, sell direct to consumers. Even after the Governor and his underlings had taken their percentage, the profit was still higher.

The most effective exploiter of the Carolina connection was Blackbeard. For nearly two years, until his death in November 1718, he led a small fleet which raided shipping in the Caribbean and off Virginia and the Carolinas. Charleston was blockaded for several weeks, during which the medicine chest incident occurred. Nothing is known for certain about Blackbeard's early life. Charles Leslie, the eighteenth-century historian of Jamaica, says he was born there 'of very creditable parents' and that his brother was an artillery captain in the Jamaican militia. Defoe says he was born in Bristol. His real name is sometimes given as Teach, sometimes as Tache or Thatch.

The crews of Blackbeard's and ~ane's vessels carousing on the ~ast of Carolina': a distinctly ~ictorian view of pirate revels, ~om The Pirates' Own Book.

In official records he appears as Tach, Tatch or Thatch, and also seems to have been known as Drummond on occasion. Defoe states that he was of giant stature and a supreme artist in histrionic terror, for 'in the commonwealth of pirates he who goes the greatest length of wickedness is looked upon with a kind of envy amongst them as a person of extraordinary gallantry. . . . Our hero assumed the cognomen of Blackbeard from that large quantity of hair which like a frightful meteor covered his whole face and frightened America more than any comet that has appeared there in a long time. This beard was black, which he suffered to grow to an extravagant length and right up to his eyes. He was accustomed to twist it with ribbons in small tails, after the manner of our Ramillies wigs, and twist them about his ears. In time of action he wore a sling over his shoulders, with three brace of pistols hanging in holsters like bandoliers; and stuck lighted matches* under his hat, which appearing on each side of his face, his eyes naturally looking fierce and wild, made him altogether such a figure that imagination cannot form an idea of a Fury from Hell to look more frightful.'

Defoe insists that Blackbeard's 'humours and passions' were suited to his appearance and gives examples of some 'frolics of wickedness so extravagant as if he aimed at making his men believe he was a devil incarnate. . . . Being one day at sea and a little flushed with drink, *Come*, he says, *let us make a hell of our own and try how long we can bear it*. Accordingly he, with two or three others, went down into the hold, and closing up all the hatches, filled several pots full of brimstone and other combustible matter, and set it on fire, and so continued until they were almost suffocated, when some of the men cried out for air. At length he opened the hatches, not a little pleased he had held out longest.' Another time, 'drinking in his cabin with Israel Hands, the master, and the pilot, Blackbeard, without any provocation, privately draws out a small pair of pistols, cocks them under the table, blows out the candle, and crossing his hands' (was this a sort of drunken pun?) 'discharges them. . . . Hands' (who was pardoned, ended his days begging in the streets of London, and may have been the original of Blind Pew in *Treasure Island*) 'was shot through the knee and lamed for life. The other pistol did no execution. Being asked the meaning of this, he answered, *That if he did not now and then kill one of them, they would forget who he was*.'

Defoe spices up the *grand guignol* by picturing Teach as a Rasputin-like, almost assassin-proof monster ('he fought with great fury till he received five-and-twenty wounds, five of them by shot'), and by quotations from Blackbeard's journal. There were, he says, 'several memorandums of the following nature, found writ with his

---

*These gunners' matches, lengths of loosely-twisted hemp cord dipped in a solution of saltpetre and lime-water, burned slowly at the rate of about twelve inches an hour.

own hand: *Such a day, rum all out – Our company somewhat sober – A dam'd confusion amongst us! – Rogues a-plotting – Great talk of separation – So I looked sharp for a prize – Took one with a great deal of liquor on board, so kept the company hot, damned hot; then all things went well again'.*

Yet for a crew of 'reprobates who encouraged and spirited one another up in wickedness' by 'a continual course of drinking', Blackbeard's company functioned with remarkable efficiency. He seems to have treated his men with the kind of mad, liquored arrogance which eighteenth-century English aristocrats commonly showed towards their servants. The Blackbeard legend ensured that no prize offered resistance, and this was presumably accepted by his crew as offsetting his lethally freakish whims. The only two engagements in which he is known to have been involved were both with naval patrol ships – the first when, no doubt much to his surprise, his flagship (a captured French slaver which he patriotically renamed the *Queen Anne's Revenge*) had to fight off an attack by HMS *Scarborough*; the second when Lieutenant Maynard of HMS *Pearl* finally caught and killed him in the James River. Official statements by the officers of merchantmen held up and rifled by Blackbeard show that he did not physically ill-treat prisoners, however much he may have blustered and blasphemed.

The treatment of captured officers depended on how they had treated their crews. Like other pirates, who combined rough justice with robbery, Blackbeard's company no doubt punished – sometimes by a running of the gauntlet, sometimes by a public flogging, very occasionally by hanging – officers who had shown particular brutality. They did not usually touch the personal possessions of officers (if they were given a good report) and men, took only what they needed from a cargo, and behaved generously to co-operative crews. 'It is a common practice with these rovers upon the pillage of a ship', wrote Governor Spotswood, 'to make presents of other commodities to such masters as they take a fancy to, in lieu of what they have plundered them of.' This was good recruiting policy and good propaganda.

At Bath Town, North Carolina, Governor Eden was bribed into complicity and the Vice-Admiralty Court found some way of legalizing prizes, as when 'though Teach had never any commission and the sloop belonged to English merchants and was taken in time of peace, yet she was condemned as a prize taken from the Spaniards'. Eden is said to have married Blackbeard to a local girl of sixteen. 'And this, as I have been informed,' adds Defoe, 'made Teach's fourteenth wife, whereof about a dozen might still be living. His behaviour in this state was somewhat extraordinary; for while his sloop lay in Ocracoke Inlet, he was ashore at a plantation where his wife lived, with whom, after he had lain all night, it was his custom to invite five or six of his brutal companions and force her to prostitute herself to them all, one after another, before his face.'

Despite his ferocious façade, Blackbeard was not a particularly bloodthirsty – or successful – pirate.

Voyeur, bully and dipsomaniac, Blackbeard at least shared everything with his comrades. Having roystered around Bath and Charleston, spending freely, he would then – no doubt to the delight of what
Defoe might have called the dregs of the populace – lead his men in
good-time raids on planters' mansions. 'Sometimes he made them
presents of rum and sugar in recompense for what he took from
them; but as for liberties which, 'tis said, he and his companions took
with the wives and daughters of the planters, I cannot take upon me
to say whether he paid them *ad valorem* or no. At other times he
carried it in a lordly manner towards them and would lay them under
contribution; nay, he often proceeded to bully the Governor . . . but it
seemed only to be done to show he dared it.' Since Governor Eden
had not the means, even if he had the will, to halt Blackbeard's
rampage, Governor Spotswood finally exceeded *his* commission by
sending HMS *Pearl* and *Lyme* to surprise the pirate in Ocracoke
Inlet. It was a strange and almost farcical dénouement, for all the
ships involved ran aground at low tide and had to jettison water casks
and ballast before they could be refloated. As the moment of truth
drew near, Blackbeard 'took a glass of liquor and drank to Lt.
Maynard saying: *Damnation seize my soul if I give or take any
quarter!*' His cargo of sugar, cocoa, indigo and cotton, seized from a
French ship off Bermuda, was impounded and valued, together with
the two sloops, at £2,500. After four years of litigation the proceeds
were shared out; but long before that the seamen who had 'fought so
valiantly against Blackbeard' (for a considerable bonus) had lost
patience and gone on the account themselves.

Blackbeard was dead, but the legend of his two-year reign of
impudent terror lived on. He was the only New Providencer to be the
subject of a ballad (sung to the tune of *What is Greater Joy and
Pleasure*):

Have you heard of Teach the Rover
And his knavery on the Main,
How of gold he was a lover
How he loved all ill-got gain?

. . . And returned, as I tell you,
To his robbery as before,
Burning, sinking ships of value,
Filling them with purple gore . . .

When the bloody fight was over,
We're informed in a letter writ,
Teach's head was made a cover
To the jackstaff of the ship.

Thus they sailed to Virginia
And when they the story told
How they killed the pirates many,
They'd applause from young and old.

By the nineteenth century he was the Pirate King of stage spectaculars and the penny-plain-tuppence-coloured cardboard theatre, and the villain of *The Black Pirate, or The Phantom Ship*, published in London in 1848 and advertised as 'A Romance of Deep Interest'.

Teach's talent as an impresario and self-publicist has overshadowed the fact that many of his contemporaries were at least as resourceful and resilient. Charles Vane, having been deposed and marooned 'with about twelve more lewd fellows who had squandered all their money got by former villainies', began again in a canoe and within six months was flourishing, with a tally of seven prizes (mainly English) and a crew of seventy-five. Rackham, surprised by a *guarda-costa* in a bay on the north coast of Cuba, where he and his company had 'stayed a considerable time living ashore with their Delilahs', led his men in a night attack on an English ship captured by the Spaniards, cut the cable, and sailed away unobserved. When day broke, the *guarda-costa* 'made a furious fire upon the empty sloop; but it was not long before they were rightly apprized of the matter, and cursed themselves for fools, to be bit out of a good, rich prize, as she proved to be, and to have nothing but an old crazy hull in the room of her'. But Charles Bellamy, who had been with Vane in the celebrated salvaged-treasure snatch, emerges as perhaps the finest flower of New Providence anarchism. He is credited with the following speech to a captain who had refused his invitation to join the pirates: 'Damn my blood, . . . you are a sneaking puppy, and so are all those who will submit to be governed by Laws which rich men have made for their own security, for the cowardly whelps have not the courage otherwise to defend what they get by their knavery. . . . They vilify us, the scoundrels, when there is only this difference, they rob the poor under the cover of Law, forsooth, and we plunder the rich under the protection of our own courage. Had you not better make one of us than sneak after the arses of these villains for employment? I am a free prince and I have as much authority to make war on the whole world as he who has a hundred sail of ships at sea. . . . But there is no reasoning with such snivelling puppies, who allow superiors to kick them about deck at pleasure and pin their faith upon a pimp of a parson, a squab who neither practices nor believes what he puts upon the chuckle-headed fools he preaches to.'

In 1718 the New Providence republic began to break up as suddenly and casually as it had been slung together. Some pirates scattered to smaller islands; since prizes were scarcer, others went on the account in the Gulf of Guinea or, drawn by tales of rich loot in the Indian Ocean and the Red Sea, rounded the Cape of Good Hope to join the pirate communities in Madagascar. The arrival at Nassau in July 1718 of a new Governor from England, escorted by two naval frigates and offering a full pardon to all the remaining miscreants if they abandoned their wicked ways, completed the process of disintegration. The Governor, Woodes Rogers, a formidable ex-privateer captain, had with six partners acquired a twenty-one-year

lease of the Bahamas from the neglectful Lords Proprietors. His post carried no salary and the islands had no source of income except piracy, which he was commissioned to suppress. In 1721 Woodes Rogers, 'Captain-General and Governor-in-Chief in and over our Bahama Islands in America', returned to England worn out with 'the dangers, troubles and fatigues' of the job, was declared bankrupt and sent to a debtor's prison. But in those three years he had shown himself to be at least as ingenious as the pirates and a good deal firmer of purpose. His expeditionary force, scraped together in England, consisted mostly of wounded veterans of Marlborough's campaigns from the Royal Hospital at Chelsea: and when the frigates left, Rogers was faced with a very difficult assignment.

Vane, who had fought his way out of the harbour, threatened to return and restore pirate rule. Using the time-honoured Spanish invasion scare, Rogers managed to enlist the services of some unemployed corsairs to put the defences in order: but he had to

Captain Woodes Rogers supervises his privateers as they politely frisk Spanish ladies for hidden jewels and gold chains at Guayaquil, Peru, in 1709.

supervise the work himself and take his turn with pick and shovel, while constantly emphasizing that the fortifications were intended to keep out papist scoundrels, for 'it was as bad as treason in England to declare our design was to keep out the pirates'. This burst of energy was followed by a lapse into lethargy. Few men were attracted by Rogers's offer of a generous 'grant' of land (which they still regarded as theirs) on condition that they built a permanent dwelling upon it. 'Work they mortally hate,' wrote Rogers, 'for when they have cleared a patch that will supply them with potatoes and yams, fish being so plentiful they thus live, poorly and indolently, and pray for wrecks or pirates.'

Within a few months, however, Rogers had won over some influential allies, including Blackbeard's old chief Benjamin Hornigold, who was commissioned as a 'privateer' to seek out Vane, Stede Bonnet, and other persistent offenders. Nothing more was seen of Vane, probably because he had lost interest, but Hornigold did bring in another privateer whose crew had mutinied and, in Defoe's phrase, 'returned to their vomit'. Though he was not empowered to pass sentence, Rogers set up a court with a jury that included several ex-pirates. Ten men were hanged, with the island militia surrounding the gallows. William Lewis, a former prize-fighter, did his best to keep up the Blackbeard tradition by calling for a tumbler of rum, and Denis Macarty, decked out in ribbons, kicked his silver-buckled shoes into the crowd. None of the condemned showed any desire to be marooned in Rogers's commonwealth, where religious tracts were distributed more freely than rumfustian and the virtues of thrift and honest labour were incessantly extolled.

Woodes Rogers returned to Nassau as Governor in 1728, this time on a salary and affluent and respected enough to sit with his family for a portrait by Hogarth. He died in 1732 in a cleaned-up town more noted for churches than taverns and full of reformed (or resigned) rogues of the kind who in their unregenerate days had made the captain of a merchantman laugh 'notwithstanding the melancholy situation I was in': for in rummaging his cabin 'they had met with a leather powder bag and puff, with which they had powdered themselves from head to foot, walked the decks with their tricorn hats under their arms, minced their oaths, and affected all the airs of a beau, with an awkwardness that would have forced a smile from a cynic'. This incident had been preceded by an incident that upset some of the captive officer's preconceived ideas. After seeing the gunner knock him unconscious with a flat-of-the-cutlass blow, the pirate captain 'resented this treatment of me so far that he got into his yawl and put off from his ship, swearing he would not sail with men who so barbarously abused their prisoners. He, however, returned on board at their persuasions and on their promise that nothing like it should happen for the future.'

There are other indications that a calculatedly horrendous façade concealed a number of rough diamonds who made up in aggregate the most remarkable treasure in the Caribbean of that time, and perhaps of any time since Columbus blundered into those seas: men who enjoyed robbing their betters but could have taught many of them a thing or two about moral courage.

William Hogarth painted this portrait of Woodes Rogers in 1729 when the ex-privateer was Governor of the Bahamas.

Madagascar and the Guinea Coast

Chapter Six **The Pirate Round**

There was nothing new about piracy in eastern waters. All through the Middle Ages, corsairs from the Malabar coast had prowled the Arabian Sea, and by the seventeenth century Mauritius and Madagascar were being used as bases by an international array of rovers. Dutch and French ships lurked in the Mozambique Channel; Portuguese pirates were established in Table Bay; Danish freebooters sailed south from the Red Sea on the 'pirate wind'. In 1616 Sir Robert Rich financed a plunder voyage in partnership with a Genoese merchant resident in London. This was followed by the ravages of the royal pirates sailing with commissions from James I and Charles I. In 1637, after a two-year cruise (with a royal licence to plunder 'from the Cape to China and Japan, including the Red Sea, the Persian Gulf and the Coromandel Coast'), the *Roebuck* and the *Samaritan* returned to England with loot worth £40,000. Captain Cobb of the *Roebuck* showed such persistence and ingenuity that the raids became known as 'Cobb's pranks'. The cruise has one other distinction. David Jones, mate and for a time acting captain of the *Roebuck*, was much given to scuttling rifled ships, and probably inspired the phrase 'Davy Jones's locker'.

But systematic piracy in the Indian Ocean, with Madagascar as a regular base, began in the 1690s. The East India Company's naval defence force, itself known as the Bombay Buccaneers, was not powerful enough to be effective against European pirates. News of this – and of the fat prizes to be taken from the East Indiamen and from Mogul and Arab vessels plying between India and the Red Sea ports of Jedda and Mocha – caused a re-think among the buccaneers who had already cultivated connections in New York, Boston and Rhode Island. At the same time, English attempts to create a trade and carrying monopoly with a series of Navigation Acts – part of the prelude to the Boston Tea Party and the war of independence – brought a boom in smuggling and increased the attractions of piracy for enterprising American colonists.

Edward Randolph, who as Surveyor-General of the Customs in New England had for twenty years been sending back reports and recommendations, summed up the situation in a memorandum of 1696 entitled *A Discourse About Pirates, With Proper Remedies to Suppress Them*. 'In the 1670s,' he wrote, 'I observed that they fitted out vessels of 60 or 70 tons which they called privateers and sent them without commission to the Spanish West Indies, whence they brought home great quantities of silver coins and bullion, with rich capes, church plate and other riches, insomuch that the Spanish

An East Indiaman prepares to sail from England, c. 1620.

ambassador complained thereof . . . but now these pirates have found out a more profitable and less hazardous voyage to the Red Sea, where they take from the Moors all they have without resistance and bring it to some one of the plantations in the continent of America or islands adjacent, where they are received and harboured and from whence also they fit out their vessels. . . . Rhode Island has been many years and still is the chief refuge for pirates. In April 1694 Thomas Tew brought in £100,000 in gold and silver and a good parcel of elephants' teeth bought up by the merchants of Boston. . . . He soon after returned to the Red Sea, and upon such great encouragement three other vessels were fitted out to join him.'

The ports of New England were kept busy building vessels for the Red Sea 'trade' or Pirate Round, as it was called, and there was brisk competition for experienced crews. Governors sold commissions (they cost £200–£300) authorizing attacks on French shipping and 'installations', usually on the Guinea Coast. But when the 'privateers' returned with plunder from the East, no awkward questions were asked. Everyone was happy except the 'Moors', and they were only heathen.

The Round operated so smoothly during the decade or so of its existence that pirates went in for domesticity and sometimes offered wives and children as pledges of their return. There was little need for such hostages, who would probably have been abandoned without qualm anyway if better business arrangements had been available; but with every possible facility and security provided, there was no inducement to double-cross. Even after financiers and Governors had taken their very substantial cuts (up to forty or fifty per cent), the returns were still far greater than any since the days of the luckier Elizabethan corsairs or Old Guard buccaneers.

In *Piracy Destroy'd*, a pamphlet published in 1701, an East India Company official claimed that 'this so successful and undisturbed piracy in the East rang so in the ears of those that with small success were privateering against the French that whole companies both from England and our American colonies flocked thither'. For the first time since Jamaica was occupied in 1655 the government found it hard to get men to serve on privateers, and the pirates had no difficulty luring crews of Royal Africa and East India Company ships from their very precarious allegiance. Like New Providence, Madagascar had fine natural harbours, security for careening, ample fresh water and provisions – including citrus fruits to combat scurvy: 'Gone to Madagascar for Limes' was a message often left behind at other rendezvous. Incessant fighting between primitively-armed tribes gave the pirates a chance to carve out 'kingdoms' of their own. A few Europeans with firearms were worth an army, and their efforts were rewarded with a grant of half the prisoners of war, who were sold to slavers. Some pirates set up as traders, notably Adam Baldridge, who from 1690 to 1697 acted as agent for a New England syndicate. His post on St Mary's Island, with its warehouses and

GOA.

Carolus Allard excudit. Cum Priv. ord. Holl. et Westfr.

A view of Goa, the Portuguese trading centre on the west coast of India, in 1667. Carracks sailing from here offered rich prizes to rovers of the Pirate Round and freebooters from Madagascar.

fortress, was situated on one of the best harbours, and soon became the favourite base for pirate cruisers and a refuge for shipwrecked seamen, maroons and deserters.

Baldridge, who kept a journal, watched pirate companies sharing their plunder. 'October 1691. Arrived the *Bachelor's Delight*, Captain George Rayner, 180 tons or thereabouts, 14 guns, 80 men, that had taken a ship belonging to the Moors. They took so much money as made the whole share run about £1,100 per man. They careened at St Mary's and I supplied them with cattle for their present spending. . . . They gave me for my cattle a quantity of beads, five great guns for a fortification, some powder and shot, six barrels of flour, and about 70 bars of iron. The ship belonged to Jamaica and set sail for Port Dauphin in Madagascar to take in their provisions . . . December 9th they sailed for Carolina.'

Tew's expedition was equally successful. Baldridge checked in his ship, the *Amity*, in October 1693, and estimated the share-out at £1,200 per man. Tew, a very experienced operator, came from Rhode Island. The cruise of the *Amity* had begun towards the end of 1692, with a commission from Isaac Richier, Governor of Bermuda, to help the Royal Africa Company in an expedition against a French factory (trading post) in Guinea. Tew had bought a share in the ship, which was owned by a syndicate of merchants and officials (including members of the Bermuda Council) and crewed by veteran buccaneers. The commission was a routine Pirate Round spoof. Everyone knew the form, and there was no need for Tew to call the company together and persuade them to forget about the Royal Africa Company, as Defoe relates. Yet his version is worth quoting because of the way it epitomizes pirate logic, or casuistry. Tew describes the Guinea expedition as a wash-out, 'for if they succeeded they would do no service to the public, advantaging only a private company from which they could expect no proper reward for their bravery'. He assumes that none of his audience is fond of fighting for its own sake, and proposes 'one bold push that would do their business. . . . The crew finding that he expected their resolution, cried out one and all, *A gold chain or a wooden leg, we'll stand by you.*'

They were not inclined to push their luck. After one prize had exceeded all expectations the quartermaster ('who is like the Grand Mufti among the Turks'), having consulted the men, vetoed any further forays. On his return, Tew is reported to have 'been received and caressed by Governor Fletcher (of New York), dining and supping with him and appearing publicly in his court', where Tew's wife and daughters glittered in diamonds and silks. After spending the summer of 1694 in Newport while the *Amity* was refitted, Tew bought a new commission from Fletcher and sailed again in November. Three months later he joined forces in the Red Sea with the 'Arch Pirate'. Defoe called this man John Avery, but he signed himself Henry Every and is so named in the Calendar of State Papers and in contemporary ballads:

Come all you brave boys whose courage is bold
Will you venture with me? I'll glut you with gold.
Make haste unto Corunna; a ship you will find
That's called the *Fancy*, will pleasure your mind.

Captain Every is in her and calls her his own;
He will box her about, boys, before he has done:
French, Spaniard and Portuguese, the heathen likewise,
He has made war with them until that he dies. . . .

Farewell fair Plymouth, and Cat-Down be damn'd:
I once was part owner of most of that land:
But as I'm disownèd so I'll abdicate
My person from England to attend on my fate.

Then away from this climate and temperate zone,
To one that's more torrid you'll hear that I'm gone
With a hundred and fifty brave sparks of this age
Who are fully resolved their foes to engage. . . .

My commission is large and I made it myself,
And the capstan shall stretch it full larger by half;
It was dated in Corunna, believe it my friend,
From the year ninety-four unto the world's end.

I honour St George and his colours I wear,
Good quarters I give but no nation I spare;
The world must assist me with what I do want –
I'll give them my bill when my money is scant. . . .

To his intimates Every was known as Long Ben, though Defoe describes him as 'middle-sized, inclinable to be fat, and of a jolly complexion'. A contemporary pamphlet makes him the son of John Every or Avery, a prosperous tavern-keeper near Plymouth, who wanted him to be a scholar; 'but instead of learning his books he became vicious and could swear to any point of the compass'. The boy is kidnapped by drunken sailors and taken on board a merchant-man, where he becomes quite a favourite, sleeping in 'a little hammock slung in the captain's own cabin'. In Carolina he is sold to a merchant who takes pity on him and sends him to college. Still a reluctant pupil, he is shipped back to Plymouth, takes to thieving and finds it advisable to go to sea again, 'where in time he became as famous for robbing as Cromwell for rebellion'.

Cross-questioned in court, a Dutchman who had sailed with Every described him as an honest seaman who served first in the navy, then in the merchant marine, before turning to piracy. In 1693 a Royal Africa Company officer reported that 'he had never found the negroes so shy and scarce' and attributed this to 'the kidnapping tricks of Long Ben, alias Every, and others of his kidney' – probably unlicensed slavers – 'who had seized them off without any payment'. At this time it seems that Every was under the protection of Governor Jones of the Bahamas. He is next heard of as sailing master on the *Charles II*, a Bristol privateer hired by the Spanish government in 1694. She was ordered to the Caribbean to help break up an illicit trade with the Spanish colonies carried on by French smugglers based on Martinique. Soon after putting in to La Coruña to pick up provisions and passengers, the crew mutinied, elected Every captain, and rechristened their ship the *Fancy*.

The *Fancy* turned up at Madagascar after some desultory pillaging around the Cape Verde Islands. At the island of Johanna in the Comoro Gulf she took her first considerable prize, a French pirate crammed with Moorish booty, and signed on most of the crew. Before leaving Johanna in February 1695 Every wrote an open letter which was picked up by an East Indiaman and taken to London: 'To all English Commanders', it began, 'I was riding here in the *Fancy*, man-of-war, formerly the *Charles* of the Spanish Expedition . . . being then and now a ship of 46 guns, 150 men, and bound to seek our fortunes. I have never yet wronged any English or Dutch, nor ever intend whilst I am commander. . . . If you or any whom you may inform are desirous to know what we are at a distance, then make your ancient [ensign] up in a ball or bundle and hoist him at the mizen peak, the mizen being furled. I shall answer with the same, and never molest you, but my men are hungry, stout, and resolute, and should they exceed my desire I cannot help myself. . . . As yet an Englishman's friend . . . Henry Every'.

The *Fancy* had been joined at Johanna by two regular Roundsmen, and while they were lurking at the entrance to the Red Sea for the Mocha fleet two more – one of them the *Amity* – hove in sight. Every was given temporary command of this formidable squadron. All but two ships of the Mocha fleet slipped past the watchers during the night, making for Surat. Engaging the smaller straggler, the *Fateh Mahomed*, Tew was killed 'by a great shot' (Baldridge's journal); but the *Amity* continued her cruise, putting in at St Mary's Island in December.

Meanwhile the *Fancy*, having captured the *Fateh Mohamed*, pursued the *Gang-i-sawai* (anglice *Gunsway*), a much larger ship of sixty-two guns with four hundred soldiers aboard, which Khafi Khan, an Indian historian, rated 'the greatest in all the Mogul dominions'. She offered a very feeble resistance. Khafi Khan's account of the subsequent orgy of rape and pillage is confirmed by an East India Company despatch. The pirates 'did do very barbarously by the passengers to make them confess where their money was, and there happened to be a great umbraw's wife related to the Great Mogul, returning from a pilgrimage to Mecca in her old age. She they abused very much and forced several other women, which caused one person of quality, his wife, and nurse to kill themselves to prevent the

Henry ('Long Ben') Every, a Plymouth man whose plunderi[ng] of Mogul ships in the Indian Ocean in 1696 earned him the title of 'Arch Pirate'.

husband's seeing them (and their being) ravished.' A crewman on the *Fancy* who later turned King's evidence confirmed that many women jumped overboard, while others died after being brutally raped. 'We took', he remembered, 'great quantities of jewels and a saddle and bridle set with rubies designed as a present for the Great Mogul.'

This was one of the most glittering pirate hauls of all time. The five ships' companies involved must have totalled around four hundred men: yet Every's crew 'took out so much in gold and silver in coined money and plate as made each man's share £1,000' (as 'Admiral' Every took a double share and the other captains a share and a half). The squadron now separated. On the *Fancy* there was a heated argument about which part of America to make for, since as Pirate Round outsiders they had no regular colonial base. Every had to outface a mutiny before getting agreement for his plan to try the Bahamas first; and those who wanted to stay behind were put ashore. In April 1696 the *Fancy* sailed from Madagascar with a crew of just over a hundred.

Company officials predicted that Every's exploit would 'raise a black cloud at court, which we wish may not produce a severe storm'. In fact news of the *Gunsway* incident provoked the worst reprisals the Company had yet known. In Surat and Agra crowds besieged the homes of English residents. One agent was stoned, others put in irons and jailed. Indian troops surrounded the Company's factory in Bombay until money and goods had been removed to compensate the Mogul's subjects for their losses. The English government put a price of £500 on Every's head, and the Company doubled the reward.

Every had flown a gaudy personal pennant in the Indian Ocean, and when news of the great *Gunsway* capture reached London the balladeers rushed romantically into print:

Now this I do say and solemnly swear,
He that strikes to St George the better shall fare,
But he that refuses shall suddenly spy
Strange colours aboard of my *Fancy* to fly

Four chivileges of gold in a bloody field,
Environ'd with green, now this is my shield,
Yet call out for quarters before you do see
A bloody flag out, which is our decree

No quarters to give, no quarters to take,
We save nothing living: alas! 'tis too late,
For we are now sworn by the bread and the wine,
More serious we are than any divine. . . .

In the Caribbean, calling first at the Danish island of St Thomas, the *Fancy* left a trail of cut-price loot and satisfied customers. Père Labat, a Jesuit priest, noted in his journal: 'A roll of muslin

The docks at Bristol, one of the main centres of privateering and the slave trade. Several celebrated pirates – including Every and Bartholomew Roberts – served on slavers and privateers before going 'on the account'.

embroidered with gold could be obtained for only 20 sols and the rest of the cargo in proportion. . . . Many merchants in St Thomas had filled their stores with these Indian stuffs and sold them more cheaply than the merchants in Martinique. . . . I used all the money I had and 200 écus that I borrowed, to buy as much of these materials as I could.' Nicholas Trott, Governor of the Bahamas, accepted a huge bribe – two thousand pieces of eight and ivory and other goods worth £7,000 – to let the pirates ashore, but he was not empowered to issue a pardon. On 15 June 1696 the Governor of Jamaica wrote virtuously to the Council for Trade and Plantations: 'The pirates that ran away from Corunna have been in the Red Sea and gotten great wealth, up to £300,000 it is reported. They are arrived at Providence and have sent to try if they could prevail with me to pardon them. . . . I was told that it should be worth to me a *great gun* [i.e. £20,000], but that could not tempt me from my duty.'

The company broke up and scattered. Some went to the Carolinas and New England where, after more official palms had been greased, they were absorbed into the pool of pirates on call for the Round. (Governor Fletcher bullied the Council in New Jersey to issue pardons, and Governor Markham of Philadelphia married his daughter Jane to one of Every's men.) Others stayed in the West Indies. Every changed his name to Bridgeman and sailed for Ireland with twenty men in the sloop *Seaflower*. After landing at Dunfarghy in Donegal, he vanished. One of his mates who was captured said he had gone to Scotland; another that he had expressed his intention of returning to Plymouth; another that he was living in London. Defoe, determined to clear up the mystery and give his story a suitably cautionary end, claimed that Every had died penniless in Bideford, cursing the Bristol fences (who had taken his jewels and cheated him of payment) as 'greater pirates than any he had known'.

Jewellers and goldsmiths in London and most of the larger towns had been warned to report any suspicious persons offering gems and foreign gold coins for sale, and they turned in some of the smaller fry. John Dann was arrested in Rochester, his home town, 'by means of a maid who found his gold quilted up in his jacket' and sneaked off to tell the mayor. Citizens of Westport, County Mayo, were astonished that the *Isaac*, a thirty-ton sloop, should have as cargo nothing but chests of gold and silver, and amazed when the mariners offered enormous sums 'for nags not worth ten shillings'. Some were arrested in the taverns, others on their way across Ireland making for Bristol or London. A broadsheet of the time – *Villany Rewarded: or The Pirate's Last Farewel to the World* – spelled out clearly the obvious lesson:

Thus wickedly we every day liv'd upon others' good,
The which, alas! we must repay now with our dearest blood;
For we on no one mercy took, nor any did we spare.
How can we then for mercy look? Let pirates then take care. . . .

But Every was never captured. Pamphlets pictured him in Madagascar suffering 'the horrors and dread of an awakened conscience' and, frenzied by the knowledge that he had no way to dispose of his treasure, 'making several offers to some men in power of very large amounts, some say to the extent of paying the National Debts, to be allowed to come to England'. The aged if aristocratic pilgrim returning from Mecca became the Great Mogul's lovely young daughter. In some versions she had many children by Every in Madagascar, where he lived in 'great royalty and state . . . master of a stout squadron manned with able and desperate fellows of all nations'. In others he had 'ravished the young princess and the ladies of her retinue, then took her to Madagascar where she had a child by him who died in its infancy and she soon afterwards broke her heart and died'. Defoe himself dashed off a highly coloured pamphlet about Every and used him as the basis for his picaresque novel, *The Life, Adventures and Piracies of Captain Singleton* (1720). Never one to underexploit sure-fire material, Defoe may also have been the Charles Johnson who wrote *The Successful Pirate*, a play about a pirate king (Arviragus) in Madagascar, produced at Drury Lane in 1712 and denounced by a leading critic for 'making a tarpaulin and Swabber the Hero of a Tragedy'.

Edward Russell, Earl of Orford As First Lord of the Admiralty he was one of a syndicate of Whig Ministers who helped finance the ill-fated cruise of Captain Kidd.

The cruise of the *Fancy* had ended in disaster and several dozen hangings. Much of the spoil from the *Gunsway* had been scooped off by officials and informers. But the legend of the Arch Pirate and Scourge of the Indies flourished – and helped to publicize the Indian Ocean as the New Eldorado.

The most notorious attempt to imitate Every's success (with a maximum of official backing) was that of Captain Kidd and his associates. The idea was to set up a fancy Pirate Round under the auspices of the Earl of Bellomont (an Irish peer who was to replace Fletcher as Governor of New York), with a syndicate of Whig politicians (including Sir John Somers, the Lord Chancellor; Edward Russell, later the Earl of Orford, First Lord of the Admiralty; the Earl of Romney, Master of the Ordnance; and the Duke of Shrewsbury, a Secretary of State) secretly financing the venture. King William, down for the customary royal tenth, was persuaded to grant two commissions to 'our trusty and well-beloved Captain William Kidd'. One was a straightforward privateering licence to 'make purchase of' French shipping, the other a special commission to seize pirate ships and their plunder – which was expected to yield the largest dividend.

The Rules of Agreement were drawn up in London in autumn 1695 by Bellomont, Kidd (a New York shipowner) and Colonel Livingston (a New York banker), all of whom were shareholders. Kidd and Livingston – the latter contemptuously described by Fletcher as 'never disbursing sixpence but with the expectation of twelve . . . a little Book Keeper who has screwed himself into one of

the most considerable estates in the province' – had crossed the Atlantic to give evidence against Fletcher in a Board of Trade inquiry into his malpractices. Kidd's origins are a little uncertain. He was born in Scotland, probably about 1645, possibly in Greenock, the son of a Presbyterian minister. The first firm fact known about him is that he fought as a privateer captain against the French in the West Indies in 1689–91. He was said to have been a competent commander, but his crew mutinied and went on the account under the leadership of one Robert Culliford. Through marriage to a wealthy widow, Kidd acquired a comfortable estate, with an elegant mansion in Wall Street. Having done Bellomont a service by testifying against Fletcher, he pressed hard to achieve his great ambition – command of one of His Majesty's ships of war. Instead he was given command of the *Adventure Galley* and hustled off to the Indian Ocean to make cabinet ministers' fortunes by plundering pirates.

The voyage started badly. Sailing from Deptford in February 1696 Kidd, whose royal commission seems to have gone to his head, refused to dip his colours to a naval sloop, and at the Nore a press-gang came aboard and took many of his best sailors. Leaving Plymouth in April he put in to New York, made up his crew from

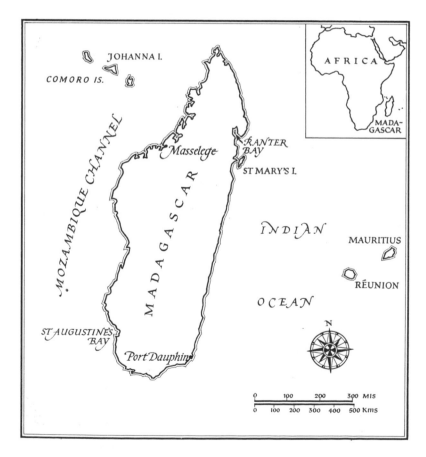

Madagascar and surrounding islands : bases of the Pirate Roundsmen.

Fletcher's pirate pool, and was forced to alter the articles in their favour, raising the company's share from 25 to 40 per cent. Fletcher revenged himself on his denouncer by writing to the Commissioners of the Board of Trade that 'many flocked to him from all parts, men of desperate fortunes and necessities, in expectation of getting vast treasure. It is generally believed here they will have money *per fas aut nefas*, and that if he misses the design named in his commission he will not be able to govern such a herd of men under no pay.'

In September the *Adventure Galley* began her nine-thousand-mile voyage. Three months later, near the Cape of Good Hope, she narrowly escaped the attentions of another press-gang from a naval squadron. Cholera and scurvy killed a third of the crew in a single week, and Kidd had to take on fifty replacements at Johanna. By this time almost his entire company were seasoned corsairs. In August 1697 an attempt to cut out a Mogul merchantman from a fleet convoyed by Dutch and English guard ships failed. The only price so far taken was a French 'banker' (fishing ship) with nothing but salt and gear in her hold, and she had been turned over to the authorities in New York. The *Galley* was leaky, the men mutinous. The crew of an Arab barque stopped and forced to hand over provisions alerted East India Company factors to the presence of 'an English pirate'. Next the *Galley* was engaged by two Portuguese *guarda-costas* near Goa and badly damaged. When Kidd refused to plunder the *Loyal Captain*, an English merchantman, his crew lost patience. During a fierce argument with William Moore, a gunner, Kidd seized a bucket and struck the man a fatal blow on the head.

Three small vessels, one Dutch (but with a French East India Company pass), one Arab, and one Portuguese, were plundered in the next few weeks to appease the mutineers – and to eat. Shortly afterwards, in February 1698, the cruise was at last made with the capture of the *Quetta Merchant* off the coast of Malabar. She was laden with gold, jewels, silks, muslins, iron and sugar, a cargo surely opulent enough to earn forgiveness for a few petty thefts and the manslaughter of an insolent gunner. True, the ship was owned by Indians, her lading was the property of Armenians, she was manned by Arabs and captained by an Englishman – but she did have a French pass, and was therefore – just – a legal as well as a lucrative prize. What more could the syndicate ask?

Kidd made the mistake – duly underlined at his trials – of breaking bulk by selling off £10,000 worth of the cargo and sharing the proceeds among his crew, who would probably have lynched him if he had not done so. Then the *Adventure Galley* (which by this time was barely seaworthy, with eight men working the pumps in hourly shifts) and the *Quetta Merchant* sailed for Madagascar. At St Mary's, by a strange coincidence, lay at anchor the *Mocha*, a former Company frigate captured and now commanded by none other than Robert Culliford, the man who had purloined Kidd's brigantine in the West Indies. Here, it seemed, was the perfect opportunity for Kidd to put himself right in the clear (and to settle an old score) by arresting a pirate. Culliford and his company of forty, seeing themselves hopelessly outnumbered and outgunned, fled ashore. The *Mocha* and whatever loot was on board were there for the taking. But Kidd's crew had other ideas. Most of them went over to Culliford and plundered the *Galley* and the *Merchant* of all that could be stowed on the *Mocha*, warning Kidd, who barricaded himself in his cabin, that if he tried to make trouble he would get a bullet in his head. They also, he claimed, burned the *Adventure Galley*'s log, thus destroying important evidence in his favour.

The *Mocha* sailed from St Mary's in June 1698, leaving Kidd to his own devices. Still hoping to beat the rap, he collected a crew of 'resting' freebooters, burned the hull of the *Galley* for its iron, and prepared the *Quetta Merchant* for the long voyage home. There was enough booty left to repay the promoters with maybe a little over for himself, and he aimed to prove that he had done his damnedest to keep within the terms of his commission. At least he still had the French passes in his possession.

Even five weary months of waiting among the assorted beach-bums of St Mary's for the north-east monsoon to waft him into the Atlantic did not shake Kidd's resolve. In November 1698 the *Merchant* sailed for the Caribbean, at about the time that a royal proclamation was published offering a free pardon to all pirates east of the Cape of Good Hope – except Kidd – and a naval squadron was being fitted out to capture the new Scourge of the Indies. In London Tory pamphleteers gleefully lampooned the Whig Cabinet as 'a Corporation of Pirates' and the government, under heavy pressure from the East India Company, denounced Kidd as 'an obnoxious pirate'. Colonial Governors from Jamaica to Massachusetts were ordered to seize him on sight. News-sheets were thick with rumours about the man who was now at the centre of one of the juiciest political scandals of the century. He was a prisoner on a French ship, about to be turned over to the grim justice of the Great Mogul; he had taken his treasure to Caledonia on the Darien Isthmus, where the desperate Scottish settlers had 'received him with all his riches'; he had offered the Governor of St Thomas a bribe of 45,000 pieces of eight for asylum.

This last guess was near the mark. Kidd, having learned on arrival in the Leeward Islands in April 1699 that he had been declared a pirate, did try to get ashore at St Thomas, but was refused. At Antigua a friend advised him to get rid of the *Quetta Merchant*. He bought a sloop called the *Antonio*, moored the *Merchant* in a remote river on the south-east coast of Hispaniola, transferred some of the plunder to the sloop, and set twenty men to guard the rest. While Kidd sailed north to Long Island (where he left some treasure chests with his friend John Gardiner), the guards sold off the *Merchant*'s cargo to passing ships and visiting merchants to the tune of £300–£400 a man.

After some efforts to negotiate with Bellomont in Boston, the loot on the *Antonio* and on Gardiner's Island, valued at £14,000, was seized and Kidd, in a frantic effort to prove his innocence, handed over the French passes to the new Governor. Bellomont immediately clapped him into jail, ignored his request to return to Hispaniola to recover £60,000 worth of plunder, and wrote to Somers describing the prisoner as 'a monster . . . there was never a greater liar or thief in the world than Kidd'. Loaded with sixteen-pound irons in a damp and freezing dungeon for six months, Kidd had to endure a New Year's Sermon by the Rev. Cotton Mather on the text 'He gets riches not by right; leaves them in the midst of his days and in his end shall be a fool,' before being transported to England in February 1700.

William Kidd : the fact that his [fa]ther was a Presbyterian [cl]ergyman inspired ballad-[w]riters and artists alike to depict [hi]m burying his Bible.

Greatly shaken in mind and body, he languished in Newgate Prison until 27 March 1701, when, still denied return of his confiscated papers, he was summoned to appear before the House of Commons. If he had pleaded that he had been framed by a pack of scoundrels in office he might have become a Tory hero, or at least a useful tool, and earned himself a pension or a sinecure. Instead – perhaps because he knew that such comforts as he enjoyed in Newgate depended on 'loyalty' to his employers – he insisted on his own honesty and that of all concerned in the affair. He seemed truculent, incoherent, and drunk. The Tories lost interest in him. 'I had thought him only a knave,' said one of them, 'but now I know him to be a fool into the bargain.'

The French passes were never produced, though an American researcher discovered them in the Public Record Office some two centuries later. On 8, 9 and 10 May 1701 Kidd stood trial – three times – at the Old Bailey knowing that the verdict was a foregone conclusion. First he was found guilty of murder – that 'being moved and seduced by the instigations of the Devil he did make an assault upon William Moore upon the high seas with a certain wooden bucket bound with iron hoops, of the value of eight pence . . . which he, the said William Kidd then and there had and held in his right hand, and did violently, feloniously, voluntarily, and of malice aforethought, beat and strike the aforesaid William Moore a little above the right ear, then and there upon the high sea and within the jurisdiction of Admiralty of England, giving the said William Moore one mortal bruise of which he did languish and die'. Then he was found guilty on two separate charges of piracy, worded with equally tortuous pedantry. Towards the end of the third trial Kidd protested that Palmer and Bradenham, two members of his crew who had turned King's evidence to save their lives, were lying rogues, and told the judge, 'It is a very hard sentence. I am the innocentest person of them all, only I have been sworn against by perjured persons.'

His appeal to Robert Harley, Speaker of the House of Commons, to be sent under guard to reclaim the (non-existent) treasure of the *Quetta Merchant*, which he now valued at £100,000, went unanswered. On 23 May he was taken from Newgate to Wapping on a black-draped cart behind a Deputy Marshal carrying over his shoulder the silver oar that was the emblem of the Admiralty Court. Reeling drunk, Kidd paid no heed to the chaplain's exhortations. Even on the scaffold his luck did not change. When he was turned off the rope broke and the hangman had to give him a second drop. After that his tarred corpse was hung in chains at Tally Point 'to serve as a greater terror to all persons from committing the like crimes'.

Kidd, who had resisted almost intolerable temptations and pressures on a nightmare cruise, was the scapegoat not only for the Whig 'Corporation of Pirates' but for Culliford, Every and dozens of others who were never caught. His execution did something to mollify the East India Company and the Great Mogul. In one of the few attempts to put his 'crime' into perspective – a contemporary squib entitled 'A Dialogue Between the Ghost of Captain Kidd and the Napper in the Strand' – he still figures as a pirate, though his trade is deemed no worse than that of a well-known kidnapper who supplies sea captains with cabin boys:

'Tis true, brother Kidd, that I live in the Strand
Where low water mark is the nearer at hand,
You are Pyrate at sea and I pyrate on land
Which nobody can deny. . . .

But for the most part he was cast as the parson's black-sheep son who – after a few feeble qualms – had broken the laws of God and man. Even his Christian name was given incorrectly, so utterly had he become a lay figure to support lay sermons:

My name was Robert Kidd when I sail'd, when I sail'd,
My name was Robert Kidd when I sail'd,
My name was Robert Kidd,
God's laws I did forbid
And so wickedly I did, when I sail'd.

I'd a Bible in my hand when I sail'd, when I sail'd,
I'd a Bible in my hand when I sail'd,
I'd a Bible in my hand
By my father's great command,
And I sunk it in the sand, when I sail'd. . . .

My topsails they did shake as I sail'd, as I sail'd,
My topsails they did shake as I sail'd,
My topsails they did shake
And the merchants they did quake
So many I did take, as I sail'd. . . .

Take warning now by me, for I must die, I must die,
Take warning now by me, for I must die,
Take warning now by me
And shun bad company,
Lest you come to hell with me, for I die.

Defoe, the Whigs' most effective political hack writer, had hardly a good word to say for poor Kidd. He was turned into a bogeyman who, until Blackbeard came along, was used to scare refractory children. His buried treasure – estimated at £1 million in a 1951 press report of yet another expedition to locate it – has been searched for in New York, Nova Scotia, Florida and Hispaniola, and he figures spookily in North American folklore. Trembling seamen watch his ship slide through the mist though there is no wind to fill the sails. Treasure-hunters whose picks strike a buried chest gibber with fear as Kidd materializes in the moonlight brandishing a cutlass. Yet there is a moving touch of mercy and insight in one of the legends about this middle-aged fall-guy. It tells of a seafaring man, his clothes forever wet with water, who calls at farmhouses near New York, asking the way to Wall Street and paying for his night's lodging with curious gold coins from the East.

Pirate Round traffic began to thin out soon after the luckless Kidd left Madagascar. The scheme of most Roundsmen is typified by Samuel Burgess, who had originally intended to make a quick fortune and go home to enjoy it in comfort – a mansion on Long Island was his dream. But there was the feeling that the English, Dutch and French East India Companies would compose their commercial squabbles long enough to take effective combined action and that the delightful collaboration with the authorities and businessmen of New England could not last much longer. Prudence seemed to dictate at least temporary retirement to the cosmopolitan communities – French, English, Dutch, Portuguese – of Madagascar. The settlements at St Mary's, Masselege, Maritain, St Augustine's and Port Dauphin must have numbered several thousand men. Headed by Burgess from New York, Nathaniel North from Bermuda, John Bowen from Rhode Island, and Abraham Samuel, a mulatto from Jamaica who set himself up as pirate king of Port Dauphin, they got along by exchanging loot and slaves for gunpowder, bullets, provisions and liquor. As they became acclimatized, life on a remote tropical isle began to seem more acceptable and memories of home became blurred. There was comradeship of a kind, crude luxury, plenty of women, and the excitement of colonial politics.

In spring 1699 a naval squadron under Commodore Warren appeared off St Mary's Island. Land-locked and bottle-necked, the harbour had been made almost impregnable during Baldridge's régime. There were forty guns in batteries, but they remained silent. When they saw the warships the pirates – and Warren estimated that there were 1,500 of them on St Mary's alone – sank some ships to block the entrance, and fled inland or across to Madagascar itself. They were less inclined than ever to fight, having acquired the profound cynicism of the expatriate and the mentality of a remittance man. Warren's squadron cruised off Madagascar for nine months and was relieved by two men-of-war which carried on the good, dull work for another year or so. It seemed that the Pirate Round, the most profitable pirate sequence yet known, had ended.

And yet the Madagascar colony did not die out completely, for the attractions of piracy were still stronger than the deterrents. The issuing of Acts of Grace was an important factor in its flux and re-flux. Edward Randolph, like others before him, had warned that the only way to destroy piracy was to maintain adequate naval patrols and keep a strict check on colonial officials. Pardons were often abused and could actually encourage men to go on the account, since they only had to wait until the next Act of Grace and were not always required to give up their loot. But the maintenance of an efficient navy, and the payment of bribe-proof salaries, was too expensive and revolutionary a proposition to be seriously considered. Governments, like the big trading companies, compromised, improvised and cheese-pared. Acts of Grace could work as snares for the unwary. Pirates often surrendered to the wrong person or at the wrong time or failed to observe some of the many small-print conditions of which they were ignorant. The nine men who were hanged with Kidd, for instance, surrendered under an Act of Grace: but the only pardon they got was forgiveness of their sins by the chaplain who saw them off at Wapping Stairs.

Such trickery was apt to be counter-productive. When Captain Bowen captured an East Indiaman he told her captain that he and his company would continue to spoil until they received in plain and untwistable language a guarantee of full and free pardon for all piracies, murders, rapes and other misdemeanours committed in England or anywhere else. In their opinion the 1698 Act had been nothing but 'a sham to entrap honest pirates': and when Commodore Warren went ashore at St Mary's to offer them a pardon under this same Act, he caused a rush for the hills rather than a rush of gratitude.

Even if pirates were captured there was a strong probability that they would not be hanged or kept out of circulation for long. Many of the temporary residents of Madagascar were deserters or recruits from merchantmen who could always plead that they had been 'forced': and since there was a chronic shortage of experienced mariners their story was likely to be swallowed. In 1696, for example, some of Culliford's men were released from jail in Bombay to crew a Company frigate trading with China. Near Sumatra they organized a mutiny, killed the captain, marooned the recalcitrant, divided the cash and other pillage, and pirated around the Indian Ocean for three years.

War in Europe meant the recall from Madagascar of naval patrols which, since all was so quiet, could be reckoned superfluous. A few more adventurers crossed the Atlantic to try their luck, notably (in 1704) Captain John Halsey of Boston, who took several fat prizes, and retired with most of his company to Madagascar. Woodes Rogers, calling at Cape Town in 1711, was told by two ex-pirates who had lived on Madagascar that unless care was taken to clear the island of pirates, 'it may be a temptation for loose straggling fellows to resort thither and make it once more a troublesome nest of freebooters.'

This was obvious enough, but the home government was too busy with the pirates of America to bother about the Indian Ocean, at least for the time being. More than a hundred pirates – including Blackbeard and Stede Bonnet – were killed in action or hanged in a few months – an unprecedented and highly deterrent death rate in this kind of war.* Ironically, all this and Woodes Rogers's taming of New Providence helped to precipitate a reoccupation of Madagascar.

In the summer of 1718 Christopher Condent, a Plymouth man, led the return to eastern seas in the *Dragon*. Putting in to Madagascar in June 1719, his company was joined by the remnants of Halsey's men and took the now traditional route to the Red Sea. One of Condent's prizes, an Arab vessel taken near Bombay, was by far the richest since the days of the Round proper, the value of the ship and cargo being estimated at thirteen lakhs of rupees or about £150,000. Luxury merchandise – silks, gold-embroidered muslins, spices of all kinds – was littered thickly over the beach at St Mary's when the company broke up after the share-out. Condent and about forty others negotiated with the Governor of Réunion for a French pardon. About twenty settled permanently on the island, and one of them, called Adam, was still there in 1770, aged 104. Defoe says that Condent married the Governor's sister-in-law and migrated to St Malo to become a wealthy shipowner.

Other New Providence companies followed closely after Condent, notably those headed by Edward England (an Irishman characterized by Defoe as 'having a great deal of good nature . . . courageous, not over-avaricious, humane, but too often over-ruled'), John Taylor and Oliver la Bouche. England, in the *Fancy*, having outdone Condent in the number of Moorish prizes taken, arrived at Johanna in consort with Taylor – an altogether more ruthless operator – in the *Victory*. There, at anchor in the bay, they found two East Indiamen, the *Cassandra* and the *Greenwich*. The *Greenwich* sheered off, but the *Cassandra*, under Captain James Macrae, prepared to fight. In an engagement that lasted several hours, thirteen of the *Cassandra*'s crew were killed and twenty-four wounded. The pirates' casualties were much heavier, and when they boarded they cut down all those who had not fled ashore. Macrae, who had a severe head wound, accepted the offer of a safe-conduct aboard the *Victory*, and after a furious argument with Taylor, England let him go free in the much-battered *Fancy* with a skeleton crew and half his original cargo. The voyage to Bombay took seven weeks, during which most of the men died of thirst. Macrae was rewarded with rapid promotion, eventually being appointed Governor of Madras – and though his salary was £500 per annum he retired after eight years with a fortune of £800,000. England, deposed and turned out of the company for his 'softness' towards Macrae, struggled back to Madagascar in an open boat, and died penniless not long after.

* Stede Bonnet, hanged at Charleston with thirty of his crew, was credited with the following abject plea to the Governor: 'I heartily beseech you will permit me to live, and I'll voluntarily put it forever beyond my power to employ my life in a wicked manner by separating all my limbs from my body, only reserving the use of my tongue to call continually on the Lord my God, and mourn all my days in sackcloth and ashes to work out confident hopes of my salvation at that great and dreadful day when all righteous souls shall receive their just rewards.'

*dward England, an Irish
aptain who died in poverty
fter being deposed for 'showing
o much humanity'.

The *Cassandra* booty was said to be worth around £75,000, but the item of most immediate value was the doctor's chest, for the pirates were all 'poxed to a great degree'. With England out of the way and mercury available to cauterize the chancres, Taylor set out in the *Victory* and the *Cassandra* on one of the most riotous and profitable cruises in the history of piracy. Two Arab dhows were captured and their captains horribly tortured, and after taking a further string of prizes, including an Indiaman, Taylor bribed his way ashore at the Dutch port of Cochin. The two ships spent the Christmas of 1720 at sea 'in carousing and forgetfulness', using up their provisions at such a rate that they reached Mauritius half-starved. Having rested and revictualled, they sailed to Réunion. There the cruise was fabulously made by the unresisted capture of a Portuguese carrack with the Conde de Ericeira, Viceroy of Goa, aboard.

Taylor accepted a large ransom for the Viceroy, abandoned his now leaky ships, and sailed away in the carrack (renamed the *Victory*) with a haul of about four million dollars' worth of diamonds and some £500,000 in specie. During a final share-out at St Mary's, each man received about £4,000 in cash and a handful of diamonds. 'Here the pirates came,' writes Defoe, 'cleaned the *Cassandra* and divided their plunder, sharing 42 small diamonds to a man, or in less proportion according to their magnitude. An ignorant or merry fellow, who had only one in this division, as being adjudged equal to 42 small, muttered very much at the lot and went and broke it in a mortar, swearing afterwards he had a better share than any of them, for he had beat it, he said, into 43 sparks.'

Some 'knocked off and stayed with their old acquaintance in Madagascar, on mutual agreements, the longest liver to take all'. Most stayed with Taylor, who, sailing in consort with La Bouche, planned a second cruise and another visit to Cochin to dispose of the diamonds, but changed his mind when he heard that a naval squadron under Commodore Thomas Matthews had rounded the Cape. Matthews found St Mary's deserted, though the beach was strewn with discarded loot, 'pepper and cloves a foot thick'. He was royally received by the pirate kings of the main island, but seems to have made little or no effort to chase any of the fourteen well-armed corsairs who, according to a Company memorandum, were still prowling the seas.

Yet his cruise was a success, perhaps because it happened to coincide with a decision that there was no point in taking unnecessary risks and that, even if Matthews's squadron was harmless enough, others would not be. News of the heavy mortality in the fight with the *Cassandra* probably helped to speed the exodus. By 1722 the second Round was over and the East India Companies free to concentrate on putting paid to native pirates. Taylor and his company went back to the West Indies. Having failed (like Every) to buy a pardon from the Governor of Jamaica, they made a deal with the Governor of Portobello, 'sitting down to spend the fruits of their dishonest industry without the least remorse or compunction'. Other companies may have followed their example, and Defoe's ironic apologia – that 'if they had known what was doing in England by the Directors of the South Sea Company, they would have had this reflection for their consolation, viz; *That whatever robberies they had committed, they were not the greatest villains at large in the world*' – might have been taken straight from the corsairs' mouths.

Chapter Seven **Welsh Wizards**

Nominally a Portuguese preserve, the Guinea Coast had been subject to sporadic visitations from Elizabethan corsairs. Prince Rupert of the Rhine, a muscular giant capable of upending a mutinous seaman and holding him head downwards over the side of a ship (though a very ineffective sea commander in other respects), turned up there early in 1652 with a small fleet of what he was pleased to call 'royalist privateers' and took a few inconsiderable Spanish and English prizes. Pirate Roundsmen made occasional raids along the coast, but not until after the New Providence clear-out did the plot really thicken.

The Guinea Coast was less hospitable than Madagascar, for the Royal Africa Company had built some forts and the Negroes, used to the ways of slavers, were not unnaturally hostile to white men. But there were plenty of creeks and offshore islands, and valuable prizes for men of determination and resource: and the record shows that the Guinea pirates were exceptionally resourceful.

In 1719 a Pembrokeshire seaman, Howell Davis from Milford Haven, became the bane of English and Portuguese shipping and settlements. His rise to fame had been something of a picaresque epic. He had sailed as mate on a slaver which had been captured by Edward England on his way from Nassau to Madagascar. According to Defoe, Davis 'resolutely answered that he would sooner be shot than sign the pirates' articles. Upon which England, pleased with his bravery, sent him and the rest of the men on board the snow [or brig], appointing him captain in the room of Skinner [who had been shot] and commanding him to pursue his voyage. He also gave him a written paper sealed up, with orders to open it when he should come to a certain latitude. . . . This was an act of grandeur like what princes practise to their admirals. . . . The paper contained a generous deed of gift of the ship and cargo to Davis and the crew, ordering him to go to Brazil [perhaps to one of England's contacts], dispose of the lading to the best advantage and make a fair and equal dividend with the rest.'

A majority of the crew refused to obey these instructions and insisted upon delivering the slaves at their original destination, Barbados. Davis was jailed for three months, but released since he could not be charged with piracy. Incensed at this unjust treatment, he made his way to New Providence, only to find that Woodes Rogers had broken up the pirate republic with a hundred invalid troops and a new Act of Grace. Rogers put him on the *Buck*, a sloop manned by ex-pirates and laden with cargo for trading with the French and Spanish islands. At Martinique Davis helped to raise a mutiny, was

chosen captain 'over a large bowl of punch', drew up articles, and
'made a short speech, the sum of which was a declaration of war
against the whole world'. After careening at Coxon's Hole, on the
east coast of Cuba, Davis and his thirty-five men took two French
prizes. The second – a fair-sized ship of twenty-four guns – was
bluffed into surrender when Davis represented the first prize as a
consort by forcing the prisoners on deck to masquerade as pirates and
'hoisting a dirty tarpaulin by way of black flag'.

The two prize ships, having been rifled, were released, and the
Buck sailed to the Cape Verde Islands, where Davis flew the English
flag and, being mistaken for an English privateer, was well received
and 'caressed by the Governor and inhabitants'. During the next five
weeks 'no diversion was wanting which the Portuguese could show or
money could purchase'. Five men stayed behind and 'one, a
Monmouthshire man, married and settled himself'. Sailing on to
Gambia, Davis, the master and the surgeon, 'dressed like gentlemen'
and posing as traders from Liverpool 'bound for the river of Senegal
to trade for gum and elephant's teeth', deceived the Governor of
Gambia Castle, took him prisoner during dinner – for which Davis
had thoughtfully provided 'a hamper of European liquor' – and made
off with a store of bar-gold and ivory. The *Buck* now fell in with two
other pirate ships, one captained by La Bouche, the other by Thomas
Cocklyn, also a refugee from New Providence. Davis was elected
commodore for a joint cruise, but declined the honour when, 'strong
liquor stirring up a spirit of discord, they quarrelled. . . . Since we met
in love, said he, let us part in love, for I find that three of a trade can
never agree.'

In the next few months Davis took seven prizes, English and
Dutch, with slaves, gold dust and ivory, abandoning the *Buck* and
transferring to a Dutch ship which he named the *Royal Rover*. One of
the prizes, captured off Anamabo within sight of the Royal Africa
Company fort at Cape Corso (Coast) Castle, was the *Princess*, a slaver
whose second mate was another Pembrokeshire man, the thirty-six-
year-old Bartholomew Roberts from Haverfordwest. Davis, who
prided himself on never forcing a man to turn pirate, took Roberts
along to give him time to make a decision and sailed east, having the
luck to seize a vessel 'with the Governor of Accra on board, with all
his effects, going to Holland'. At Prince's Island, Roberts had a good
chance to observe his fellow-Welshman's ingenuity. Again flying
English colours, Davis convinced Portuguese officials that he was in
command of a pirate-hunting naval squadron, 'hoisted out the
pinnace man-of-war fashion', and was given a military escort of
honour. His effrontery reached a zenith when he decided to plunder a
French ship that put into the harbour for supplies. 'To give the thing
a colour of right, he persuaded the Portuguese that she had been
trading with pirates and that he had found several pirates' goods on
board which he had seized for the King's use. This story passed so
well with the Governor that he commended Davis's diligence.'

Prince Rupert of the Rhine, a
dashing cavalry leader during
the English Civil War, turned
'privateer' in 1648.

Prince Rupert.

It must have seemed that the gullibility of these colonial block-heads knew no bounds, for Davis now planned 'to make a present to the Governor of a dozen negroes . . . and afterwards to invite him with the chief men and some of the friars to an entertainment. The minute they were on board they were to be secured in irons and kept till they should pay a ransom of £40,000 sterling.' But nemesis was near. One of the Negroes swam ashore during the night and revealed the plot. When the 'naval officers' landed in the morning they were ambushed and shot down. Davis was mortally wounded, but 'just as he fell he perceived he was followed, and drawing out his pistols fired them at his pursuers: thus, like a game cock, giving a dying blow that he might not perish unrevenged'.

The career of a man whose company 'had conceived so high an opinion of his conduct and courage that they thought nothing impossible to him' was over: and they turned to another Welshman in the hope that he might lead them with similar wizardry. They were not to be disappointed. Roberts, though completely eclipsed in popular legend by Every, Kidd and Blackbeard, became the most celebrated rover of his time. Defoe describes him as a tall, swarthy, handsome, fiercely proud man, a fancy dresser who, though he never touched strong liquor (preferring to drink tea), was no spoilsport. Though at first, like Howell Davis, reluctant to change his way of life, he acted with panache once he had taken the plunge. One Walter Kennedy was sent with an assault force to attack the Portuguese fort under cover of a barrage from the *Royal Rover*, which mounted thirty-two cannon and twenty-seven swivel guns. The town was bombarded and two Portuguese ships set on fire. After revictualling at the island of Anabona, it was decided by a majority vote to cruise to Brazil.

Nine weeks of hovering well out to sea produced no prizes; then, standing in to land, the *Rover* sighted a fleet of forty-two Portuguese ships newly laden for the return voyage to Lisbon, with two seventy-gun naval escorts nearby. Coming alongside one of the small vessels, Roberts invited the captain aboard and ordered him to point out the richest prize, which happened to be the *Sagrada Familia*, forty guns and 150 men. The *Rover* made straight for her, slammed in a broadside, and boarded. While the two men-of-war were upping anchor in response to gunfire signals from the other merchantmen, Roberts sailed the *Sagrada Familia* out of the fleet. It was one of the most daring pirate captures ever made, with a sumptuous yield of forty thousand moidores (about £70,000), tobacco, sugar and hides, 'besides chains and trinkets of considerable value; particularly a cross set with diamonds designed for the King of Portugal'.

After a few weeks' carousing on Devil's Island, where the Spanish Governor had no scruples about pirate booty, Roberts sailed for the West Indies, but was chased by British naval patrols and had to abandon the *Royal Rover*. He is next heard of a few months later, in June 1720, when Governor Spotswood reported that with no more

Bartholomew ('Black Bart') Roberts, whose career reached a peak with the capture of eleven sail at Whydah. His ship is flying his personal jack in defiance of the colonial Governors.

than a sloop of ten guns and 60 men, he ventured into Trepanny in Newfoundland, where there was a great number of merchant ships, upwards of 1,200 men, and forty pieces of cannon, and yet for want of courage in this heedless multitude, he plundered and burnt divers ships there and made such as he pleased prisoners'. The Boston *News Letter* described how Roberts's sloop 'went in with drums beating, trumpets sounding, English colours flying, and the pirate flag at the topmast with death's head and cutlass'; and the Lieutenant-Governor of New England remarked in his account of the incident that 'one cannot withhold admiration for his bravery and daring'.

Having mounted sixteen guns on a Bristol galley taken at Trepanny, Roberts signed on more hands* (he now had a company of a hundred), plundered ten French sail on the Banks, kept the best – a ship of twenty-six guns which he christened the *Royal Fortune* – and let the French captain have the Bristol galley in exchange. The most valuable of a further string of prizes was the *Samuel* from London, with several passengers who, according to the *News Letter*, were robbed of all their cash and clothes by pirates who 'behaved like a parcel of furies. They often made mock of King George's Acts of Grace with an oath that they had not got money enough, but when they had, if he then did grant them one after they had sent him word, they would thank him for it'.

Sensationalizing journalists alleged that Roberts tolerated 'barbarous abuse' of prisoners – 'some they almost whipped to death, others had their ears cut off, others they fixed to the yardarms and fired at them as a mark'. No doubt there were times when the company got out of hand. Roberts was more capable than most captains of enforcing the discipline that all pirate articles required, but he was never allowed to be an autocrat. Defoe states that when Roberts killed a drunken seaman who insulted him, he was set upon and thrashed by the dead man's mate until the quartermaster intervened and, 'to uphold the captain's dignity', put it to the vote that the culprit should be flogged. The fact that 'his' articles called for a ban on gambling, insisted that candles should be out by eight o'clock, and ordered that 'if any of the crew after that hour still remain inclined for drinking, they shall do it on the open deck', did not prove that Roberts was a stern disciplinarian, only that he was concerned with basic safety. Similarly, a clause stipulating that 'the musicians are to have rest on the Sabbath day' did not mean that Roberts was a 'sabbatarian' or 'puritan', only that the company agreed that everyone was entitled to a day off.

Defoe gives an almost wistful description of a pirate court-martial on the *Royal Fortune*. 'Here was the form of justice kept up, which is as much as can be said of several other courts that have more lawful commissions for what they do. Here was no feeing of counsel and

An eighteenth-century print showing fish being landed and cleaned in Canada. It was to escape this work, in miserable conditions, that hundreds of Newfoundland labourers went on the account.

---

* Bleak and sparsely settled, Newfoundland had since the late sixteenth century been a prime recruiting-ground for pirates during the cod-fishing season, when there was an influx of badly-paid 'slitters' brought over in the fishing fleets from Bristol, Barnstaple and Topsham. Defoe estimates that in 1720 there were more than a thousand of these labourers 'who during the season of business (the hardness of their labour and chilliness of the nights pinching them very much) are mostly fond of drinking Black Strap [made from rum, molasses and chowder beer]. By this the majority of them outran the constable and were necessitated to come under hard articles of servitude for their maintenance in the winter. . . . The masters residing there think advantages taken of their necessities no more than a just and lawful game. . . . Wherefore they sometimes run away in shallops and boats and begin on piratical exploits. Secondly they are visited every summer almost by some set of pirates or other.'

bribing of witnesses . . . no packing of juries . . . no perplexing the cause with unintelligible canting terms and useless distinctions; nor was their session burdened with numberless officers, the ministers of rapine and extortion. . . . The prisoners were brought forth and arraigned upon a statute of their own making.'

'*Captain Roberts' Crew carousing at Old Calabar River*' : *drunkenness and gambling, caused by sheer boredom, were a constant threat to efficiency in pirate companies*

Despite a blenching display of ferocity – black flag flying, musicians blowing and banging,* cutlasses waving, a yelling of oaths and threats – the evidence of witnesses is that Roberts was no more brutal than Blackbeard, and for the same reasons. Though he had sometimes to 'force' specialists, including musicians, he never had any trouble making up a crew, and refused to consider any applicant who was not an experienced mariner. For what it was worth – though if it came to a trial only 'artists' could use the plea of forcing with much hope of success – he was always willing to provide new recruits with an 'insurance policy' in the form of a certificate that they had joined under duress.

By September 1720 Roberts was back in the Caribbean, plundering prodigiously. 'Between the 28th and 31st of October', reported the Governor of the French Leeward Islands, 'these pirates seized, burned or sunk fifteen French and English vessels and one Dutch interloper of 42 guns at Dominica.' Evidently determined to make the authorities pay for his previous failure in these waters, Roberts put in to Basseterre Road at St Kitts and looted and burned shipping under fire from shore batteries. Shortly after this the Lieutenant-Governor of the British Leeward Islands received the following letter:

Royal Fortune, September 27th 1720

Gentlemen:
This comes expressly from me to lett you know that had you come off as you ought to a done and drank a Glass of wine with me and my Company I should not harmed the least vessell in your harbour. Farther it is not your guns you fired that affrighted me or hindered our coming ashore, but the wind not proving to our expectation. The Royall Rover you have already burnt and barbarously used some of our men, but we have now a ship as good as her and for revenge you may assure yourselves here and hereafter not to expect anything from our hands but what belongs to a pirate – as farther, Gentlemen, that poor fellow you now have in prison at Sandy Point is entirely ignorant and what he hath was gave him and so pray make conscience for once let me begg you and use that man as an honest man. . . . If we hear any otherwise you may expect not to have quarters to any of your Island.

Yours (signed) Bathll. Roberts

* This, not the provision of chamber music or the accompaniment of sea-shanties, was the musicians' most important function.

It is a letter which might have been written by a militant trade union leader, mixing class-war threats with an appeal to 'common humanity', and strongly implying that both sides have essentially the same interests and should 'get their feet under the table' to arrange matters.

Colonial authorities found themselves powerless to organize retaliation. An Anglo-French privateering expedition came to nothing when the crews mutinied, and Roberts replied to the efforts of the Governors of Martinique and Barbados to chase him by having a special jack made. It showed himself standing with each foot on a skull, one of which was labelled ABH (A Barbadian's Head), the other AMH (A Martinican's Head). In May 1721 Governor Spotswood ordered fifty-four cannon to be placed at strategic points along the coast of Virginia to repel an expected attack by 'the great pirate Roberts' – who for nine months had dominated the Caribbean with two ships (the *Royal Fortune* and the *Ranger*, a brigantine) and 150 men.

Roberts had made one attempt to leave the Caribbean, but contrary winds had forced him to return – a terrifying trip of more than two thousand miles during which food and water ran out, so that 'many of them drank their own urine, or sea water, which instead of allaying gave them an inextinguishable thirst that killed them'. The eventual return to African waters was not without incident, for the *Ranger*, captained by Thomas Anstis (who had pirated with Howell Davis), peeled off with seventy men and put back to the West Indies, hoping to arrange a pardon. But by the end of 1721 Roberts had acquired a new *Royal Fortune* (the former Royal Africa Company frigate *Onslow*) and two consorts, the *Great Ranger* and *Little Ranger*. At Whydah this squadron held eleven sail – English, French and Portuguese – to ransom for eight pounds of gold-dust apiece, and gave receipts for payment. Some were straightforward:

This is to certify to whom it may concern that we GENTLEMEN of FORTUNE have received eight pounds of Gold-dust for the ransom of the *Hardy*, Captain Dittwitt commander, so that we discharge the said ship.

Witness our hands   Batt. Roberts
this 13th of Jan. 1722   Harry Glasby

'Others', says Defoe, 'were given to the Portuguese captains in the same form; but being signed by two waggish fellows, *viz* Sutton and Sympson, they subscribed the names of Aaron Whifflingpin and Simon Tugmutton.'

A clergyman on board the *Onslow*, going to take up his duties as chaplain at Cape Corso, had been treated with similar buffoonery (why didn't he stay with the pirates with 'nothing to do but make punch and say prayers'?). But the Whydah swoop was the last success in a dazzling sequence that stretched back unbroken for over four years to the moment when Howell Davis sailed for Brazil at the quixotic bidding of Captain England. It was ended by HMS *Swallow*, a man-of-war which, after repeated requests, had been sent to protect shipping in the Gulf of Guinea. A few days after the Whydah raid the *Swallow*, commanded by Captain Chaloner Ogle, sighted Roberts's squadron anchored at Parrot Island off Cape Lopez. The pirates mistook the man-of-war for a Portuguese merchantman (she may have flown Portuguese colours). The *Great Ranger* went after her and was taken after a fierce battle in which the pirates lost ten killed and twenty wounded. While this was happening, Roberts had seized another prize well stocked with liquor. His company was for the most part dead drunk when the *Swallow* returned to Parrot Island for the day of reckoning.

The captain himself was disturbed at breakfast – 'a savoury dish of Solomon Grundy' (*salmagundi*: a highly-spiced West Indian dish). Defoe says that 'he made a gallant figure at the time of the engagement, being dressed in a rich crimson damask waistcoat and breeches, a red feather in his hat, a gold chain round his neck with a diamond cross hanging to it, a sword in his hand and two pair of pistols, hanging at the end of a silk sling flung over his shoulder. . . . He had now perhaps finished the fight very desperately if Death, who took a swift passage in a grape-shot, had not interposed and struck him directly in the throat. He settled himself on the tackles of a gun, which one Stephenson, from the helm, observing, ran to his assistance, and not perceiving him wounded, swore at him and bid him stand up and fight like a man. But when he found his mistake, he gushed into tears and wished the next shot might be his lot.'

Bartholomew Roberts was thrown overboard in all his finery, according to his own request. The pirates, half-sobered but utterly confused by the death of a leader who, like Howell Davis, had come to seem invincible and almost immortal, struck their flag and asked for quarter. The news was acclaimed by Governors in New York, Jamaica, and even Bombay – for the Indian Ocean had probably been next on Roberts's list. Captain Ogle, who was knighted for this action, took 169 prisoners to Cape Corso Castle, where the chaplain had the satisfaction of lecturing them on the error of their ways. According to Defoe there were few signs of repentance. Most of the time was spent trying to escape and 'run down the coast to raise a new company' rather than be 'hanged like a dog and sun-dried': and the few men who did respond to the chaplain's exhortations were treated as backsliders. Sutton, 'happening to be in the same irons with another prisoner . . . who read and prayed as often as became his condition, used to swear at the fellow and ask *what he proposed by so much noise and devotion? Heaven*, says the other, *I hope. Heaven, you fool*, says Sutton, *Did you ever hear of any pirates going thither? Give me Hell, it's a merrier place. I'll give Roberts a salute of thirteen guns at entrance.*' And with that, Sutton asked that the officer should either move the man or 'take his prayer book away, as a common disturber'.

When the trials began on 28 March 1722, few veteran corsairs were among the defendants. About six had served right through the Davis-Roberts sequence; two had been with Blackbeard; but the rest – including Glasby, a forced 'artist' who was the chief witness for the prosecution – had been recruited from prizes taken in the Atlantic, the Caribbean, and along the Guinea Coast during the previous eighteen months. All pleaded not guilty because they had been forced. Ninety-one were found guilty, fifty-two being hanged. The others, mostly Londoners or West Country men, got seven years' hard labour. Most of those acquitted were very recent recruits, or 'artists'. All but one of the surgeons went free, as did the musicians.*

So ended the Royal Navy's first really effective anti-piratical exercise, and the reign of the forced Welsh Wizards who had brought such wit, style and relish to the pirate trade. There were several picturesque sub-plots to the main story: that of Walter Kennedy, for instance, an Irishman who ran away in a captured sloop during Roberts's first West Indian cruise (after which Roberts did his best to exclude Irishmen from his company). Having taken some prizes, Kennedy and about twenty others decided to make for Ireland, as Every had twenty-five years earlier. 'In this company', writes Defoe, 'there was but one that pretended to any skill in navigation' (Kennedy, an ex-pickpocket and housebreaker, could neither read nor write), 'and he proved a pretender only; for shaping their course to Ireland they ran away to the north-west coast of Scotland, where they pushed the vessel into a little creek and went ashore. . . . The main gang alarmed the country wherever they came, drinking and roaring at such a rate that the people shut themselves up in their houses. . . . In other places they treated the whole village, squandering their money as if, like Aesop, they wanted to lighten their burthens. This expensive manner of living procured two of their drunken stragglers to be knocked on the head. The rest, as they drew nigh to Edinburgh, were arrested and thrown into gaol.' Two turned informer, nine were hanged. Kennedy himself got to Deptford, and prospered as a brothel-keeper until one of his whores informed on him and he went to Execution Dock in July 1721.

'Thus', concludes Defoe, 'we see what a disastrous fate ever attends the wicked and how rarely they escape the punishment due to their crimes.' He adds, however, that eight or nine pirates remained at large, and that though they must have been conscious of 'impending law, which never let them sleep well, unless drunk', they were said to have shrugged off Kennedy's fate with the comment that 'he was a sad dog and deserved what he got'. The news of the death of Roberts and the great sun-drying at Cape Corso was a powerful

---

* Robert Louis Stevenson's very close study of Defoe's *History* comes out in one of Long John Silver's reminiscences: 'It was a master surgeon, him that ampytated me – out of college and all – Latin by the bucket and what not; but he was hanged like a dog and sun-dried like the rest at Corso Castle. That was Roberts's men, that was. . . .'

Cape Corſe

Fort Royal at Manfrow

A

mid-eighteenth-century view
the Guinea Coast, dotted with
tified trading posts, including
ape Corso Castle, where
berts's men were brought to
stice.

deterrent, no doubt; but there remained a temptation to turn to crime which must be seen in the context of prevailing conditions. Kennedy's end would have been the same if he had stolen a loaf of bread. Until the penal code began to recognize that there were degrees in 'evil-doing', plenty of men continued to reason that they might as well be hanged for a sheep as a lamb. Conditions on naval and merchant ships, too, were slow to improve. Diet deficiencies largely due to pursers' profiteering caused fearful epidemics in crowded quarters, and the use of the rope's end was second nature to boatswains, boatswains' mates, and even to midshipmen who were little more than boys. During the Seven Years War 1,522 men were killed in action but nearly 150,000 were lost through disease or desertion. So roads and lanes swarmed with highwaymen and footpads, and for those who preferred the sea, smuggling, that twin of piracy, offered plenty of employment. Roberts's motto – 'a merry life and a short one' – was not just the expression of a whimsical bravado, but a piece of incontrovertible logic buttressed by everyday under-dog experience.

HORUSCE en HAREADEN BARBAROSS

The Mediterranean

Chapter Eight **Corsairs of Malta and Barbary**

While François Leclerc, Jacques Sores, Hawkins, Drake and Oxenham were challenging the Iberian monopoly of the New World, the Mediterranean was the scene of a power-struggle as fierce and complex as any it had known in the days of the Phoenician, Greek and Roman empires. The massive Arab conquests of the eighth century had been countered by the Crusades and by the Reconquista in Spain. The Spaniards, reaching out to seize the western stretches of the North African coast (known as the Barbary Coast from its native inhabitants, the semi-nomadic Berber tribes), were checked by Moorish resistance organized and led by two brilliant Turkish adventurers, the Barbarossa brothers, Aruj and Kheir-ed-Din. Around 1530 Kheir-ed-Din was appointed Regent of Algiers, which like Tunis and Tripoli now became an outlying province of the Ottoman empire, ruled by Turks and garrisoned by Turkish troops (janissaries). Kheir-ed-Din's successors, Dragut and Ochiali, led the Turks in the famous siege of Malta (1565) and at the battle of Lepanto (1571).

With Lepanto the heroic phase of the Muslim-Christian struggle was over, and the 'holy war' settled down into a regular pattern. Privateer fleets operating from the Barbary ports and Malta, English and Dutch merchantmen intent on blasting a way into the Levant trade, Spanish and Italian corsairs, all prowled the sea – with the dwindling wealth of Venice as their main quarry. The taking and re-taking, ransoming and re-ransoming of prisoners, the raids on coastlines already raided hundreds of times over hundreds of centuries, exudes an atmosphere of claustrophobic staleness unmatched even by the last period of the age of buccaneers.

Kheir-ed-Din has been mistakenly described as lecherous and barbarian, a Christian renegade pirate whose main preoccupation was to fill his harem with beautiful white women, and who died at the age of ninety worn out by sexual orgy. In fact he died in his early sixties, respected by people of all races and religions, an ambitious but abstemious man exhausted by hard work, incessant campaigning, and the cares of office. He was highly cultivated, spoke several languages (including Spanish and Italian) and was a munificent patron of the arts, and as the Sultan's admiral and ambassador he made alliances with Christian princes in traditional balance-of-power style. Insofar as the Barbary corsairs ever became bloodthirsty pirates led by treacherous renegades, they did so under the leadership of European rovers seeking new fields after the collapse of the great Elizabethan corsair boom.

*his late-seventeenth-century
Dutch engraving of the
Barbarossa (Redbeard)
others pictures them as sadistic
rate chiefs – a popular
Christian myth.*

137

When the Spanish War ended in 1603, many English, Dutch, and French seamen found themselves unemployed, suddenly changed from heroes into vagabonds and social menaces. For the customary percentage, the Barbary ports gave them protection in harbour, immunity on land, and commissions to cruise against the old enemy, Spain, with whom the Turks were still at war. Algiers, Tunis, and Sallee (in Morocco) offered bases for hundreds, perhaps thousands of very nominally Christian adventurers, some of whom 'turned Turk'. Many were 'sea-artists' – navigators, gunners, carpenters, even shipwrights – and between them they revolutionized the Mediterranean corsair industry by teaching their hosts how to build and sail ocean-going ships. These foreign mercenaries often shocked the Turks and Moors with their barbaric ways. 'The great profit that the English bring to the country,' wrote a French observer in Tunis, 'their profuse liberality and the excessive debauches in which they squander their money before leaving the town and returning to war (as they call their sea brigandage) has made them cherished by the janissaries above all other nations. They carry their swords at their side, run drunk through the town, and sleep with the wives of the Moors. In brief, every kind of licence is permitted to them by the authorities.' The foreigners brought plunder and hard-won expertise, and were tolerated as necessary evils.

Some renegades struck it rich and became in their turn promoters of the corsair round. Among these was John Ward, an ex-privateer who had begun life as a fisherman at Faversham in Kent. Disgusted by conditions and pay as a seaman on the *Lion's Whelp*, one of the few naval ships kept in commission, he was prominent in a gang of malcontents who gathered in the taverns of Portsmouth to talk nostalgically of the good old days 'when we might sing, swear, drab and kill men as freely as your cakemakers do flies; when the whole sea was our empire where we robbed at will, and the world our garden where we walked for sport'. In 1605 he and thirty others seized a barque in Portsmouth harbour and took a French merchantman at anchor off the Scilly Islands. Renaming this prize the *Little John*, Ward put in to Plymouth to make up his crew, sailed to the Mediterranean, where he made some further captures, brought his little pirate fleet to Tunis, and came to terms with the Bey.

Well served by his chief gunners, James Proctor of Southampton and John Frith of Plymouth, within a few years Ward commanded a fleet of nine or ten well-armed ships, among them a number of converted Venetian galleys and galleons. One cruise alone, made in 1607 in consort with Jan Casten, a Dutch renegade, yielded booty worth 400,000 crowns and caused near-panic on the Venetian stock exchange. The 'new men of Barbary' had become *the* pirates of the Mediterranean. Simon Danziker, a Fleming based in Algiers, prospered so rapidly – in 1608 he took more than thirty French, Dutch and English prizes off Cadiz – that in 1609 he transferred his fleet and his wealth to Marseilles. The Grand Duke of Tuscany and

Dragut directing the Turkish siege of Malta in 1565 : this struggle for control of the Mediterranean was succeeded the 'holy war' between the Christian corsairs of Malta and their Muslim counterparts in Barbary.

the Duke of Savoy offered Ward facilities at Leghorn or Villefranche, which rivalled Algiers and Tunis as 'free ports': but the Turks presumably outbid them, for Ward died at Tunis in 1622.

News from the Sea of Two Notorious Pyrates, Ward the Englishman and Dansiker the Dutchman, a chap-book published in London in 1609, gives some idea of Ward's notoriety. His life was said to be 'nothing but a continual battle and defiance with Christians'. He 'never thought of the service of God', refused to 'go to prayers in time of tempest', jeered at any who did so, and had absolutely no scruples about plundering English ships and murdering honest English seamen. 'Thus, as the sea might by experience relate his spoils and cruelty, so the Lord was an eyewitness of his drunkenness and idle prodigality.' The pamphlet reaches a crescendo of envy and self-righteous denunciation when describing the splendour of Ward's establishment ashore and afloat. He had 'a very stately house in Tunis, rich with marble and alabaster, more fit for a prince than a pirate', was 'guarded in his cabin by twelve Turks', and ranked 'equal in estimation with the godless Bashaw'. But retribution was surely at hand: 'these honours are like letters writ in the sand, which are blown away with every gust of wind'.

The Ballad of Danseker the Dutchman tells of a formidable if short-lived partnership between him and Ward:

London's *Elizabeth*
Of late these rovers taken have,
A ship well laden with rich merchandize,
The amiable *Pearl* and *Charity*,
All ships of gallant bravery ...
Of Hull the *Bonaventure*
Which was a great frequenter
And passer of the Straits to Barbary ...

Another ballad, the perennially popular *Captain Ward and the Rainbow*, shows him trying to buy a pardon from King James I. The king refuses, and when he hears that the pirate has captured some English vessels, orders the construction of 'a worthy ship', the *Rainbow*, to end his insolence. There is a spectacular (but probably apocryphal) sea fight,* and Ward vehemently denies that he has plundered English shipping:

Shoot on, shoot on, says Captain Ward,
Your sport well pleaseth me,
And he that first gives over
Shall yield unto the sea.

I never robbed an Englishman,
I love them as my own,
All my delight is for to pull
The French and Spaniards down. . . .

Barbary galleys at sea in the late seventeenth century.

Go tell the King of England,
Go tell him this from me,
If he reign King of all the Land,
I will reign King at Sea.

There is no record that Ward in fact asked or was offered a pardon. But Peter Eston, who in 1612 led a pirate fleet of twenty-five sail into the Mediterranean, not only forced the Venetian Senate to order special defence measures to protect the Adriatic against his threatened raids, but refused a pardon from James I. 'Why', he is said to

---

* The *Rainbow* was the name of one of Drake's ships in the 1587 expedition to Cadiz, and there was a ship of that name in the Jacobean navy. There is no evidence that she ever fought with Ward, though it is possible that Ward's old ship, the *Lion's Whelp*, which was sent to the Mediterranean to suppress piracy, may have. In one version of this ballad, Ward does qualify his denial of plundering English ships:

You lie, you lie, said Captain Ward,
So well as I hear you lie.
I never robb'd an Englishman,
An Englishman but three.

have asked, 'should I obey a king's orders when I am a king myself?' This corsair admiral, once a farm labourer in Somerset, had terrorized the Bristol Channel, looted the French, Flemish and Portuguese cod-fleets off Newfoundland (where he recruited several hundred English fishermen), and finally settled in Villefranche under the protection of the Duke of Savoy, purchasing a marquisate and marrying a woman of noble birth.

Henry Mainwaring, perhaps the most famous of the Jacobean pirates, refused offers from Tunis and Madrid, and was eventually to accept a pardon from King James. He began his sea career as a pirate-hunter, being commissioned in 1611 to take Eston, which he failed to do. Five years later, however, he returned to England as an authority on piracy, having gathered a wealth of first-hand experience. The son of a well-known Shropshire family, Mainwaring, who qualified as a barrister and soldiered in the Low Countries before going to sea, entered the corsair business with a flourish reminiscent of the Elizabethan gentleman adventurers. In 1612 he bought the *Resistance*, a fast vessel of 160 tons built by the master shipwright Phineas Pett, and set out with a licence to plunder Spanish shipping in the West Indies.

Instead, he sailed for the Straits of Gibraltar, and established himself at Mamurra, a port near Sallee on the Atlantic coast of Morocco, where he was well placed to raid fleets on their way back from the Indies. Like Eston, he went to Newfoundland to plunder and recruit, but on his return found that the Spanish Admiral Fajardo had seized Mamurra in his absence. Mainwaring then removed to Villefranche, and in 1616 decisively defeated a Spanish punitive expedition consisting of five warships. After this he had the choice of a free pardon from the King of Spain (coupled with the offer of a large salary to command a Spanish squadron), or a similar proposal brought by a special envoy from the court of King James. As a patriotic pirate he chose the latter, and sailed to Dover, where he and such of his company as elected to go with him were amnestied (the formula was that though he had exceeded his original commission he had 'committed no great wrong').* Knighted in 1618, Mainwaring was appointed Lieutenant of Dover Castle and Deputy Warden of the Cinque Ports, and elected MP for Dover; wrote a very well-informed *Discourse of the Beginnings, Practices and Suppression of Pirates* (which recommended that no further pardons should be issued and that captured pirates should be used as slave-labour in the royal navy); and ended his days as a Vice-Admiral.

---

* Like Sabatini's Captain Blood, Mainwaring confined his depredations to the Spaniards. Blood refused to 'make war on English ships and English lads. That would entirely ruin our prospects.' Outlaws he and his company might be, but 'we discriminate by being the enemies of Spain alone. We're not *hostis humani generis* yet, and until we become that we need not abandon hope, like others of our kind, that one day this outlawry will be lifted.'

Sir Francis Verney, another gentleman adventurer, was less fortunate than Mainwaring, Eston and Ward. Forced by his step-mother into a childhood marriage and tricked out of his inheritance by a devious settlement, he entered the Foreign Legion of Muley Sidan, pretender to the throne of Morocco. Soon after Muley Sidan's death in 1607 reports reached England that Verney had turned pirate – and Turk – in Algiers and had plundered a number of English merchantmen from Poole and Plymouth. Captured by a 'Christian' corsair from Sicily, he spent two years as a galley slave, was redeemed through the services of an English Jesuit, and died in hospital at Messina, aged thirty-one, after enlisting in the ranks of the Sicilian army. A few exotic personal effects were all that was left to show for his dreams of a Barbary fortune. They were returned to the Verney home at Claydon in Buckinghamshire and may still be seen there – a turban, two pairs of Arab slippers, and a pilgrim's staff inlaid with mother-of-pearl crosses.

The real shock came when the Barbary and Sallee rovers, equipped with ocean-going ships and renegade captains, navigators and gunners, burst out of the Mediterranean, bringing the 'Turkish peril' nearer home. Encouraged by reports of the decay of the English navy (Dunkirk corsairs were plundering coastal shipping from Newcastle to King's Lynn), they raided the south-west coast and, using Baltimore in Ireland as a base, lurked in the Bristol Channel or crossed the Atlantic to plunder the Newfoundland fleets. 'Sea artists' and slaves were their main objectives. Very occasionally, at Baltimore and in Devon and Cornwall, they raided ashore to carry off men, women and children.

In France, Italy, Spain and England, redemptionist preachers painted lurid pictures of the sufferings of Christian captives – though without mentioning that at least as many captive Turks and Moors were sold into slavery in Spain, Malta and Italy – appealing to the susceptibilities of relatives and countrymen. Barnstaple, for instance, raised the considerable sum of £240 in 1622 to redeem six local seamen who were said to be enduring 'unspeakable tortures' in Algiers. Inland villages sent contributions to a central fund. The redemptionist racket, based on the myth of the Terrible, Licentious Turk (an Algerine ship captured in the Bay of Biscay in 1622 was captained by a turbaned English renegade – 'as they say, a chandler's son in Southwark' – and crewed mostly by English, French and Dutch seamen), gave lucrative employment to a small army of middlemen, lay and ecclesiastical. The lobby of the House of Commons was often filled with the wives and offspring of Barbary prisoners. From time to time the proceeds of a small extra tax on imported goods were set aside to still their clamour, and in 1624 letters patent were granted for a nationwide collection. In the House of Lords barons subscribed twenty shillings and peers of higher rank forty shillings. The Commons resolved that every member who came late to prayers should be fined and the money put in a Barbary Widows' fund.

Only about a sixth of the £70,000 raised by this appeal was used for redemption, the rest being siphoned off by the Admiralty. Naval defence, however, was so feeble (some Sallee rovers plundered well up the Thames) that the government authorized the owners of merchant ships to keep all the takings from any 'privateering' seizures; and the Elder Brethren of Trinity House ordered the Lizard Light, set up in 1588, to be extinguished because 'it will conduct pirates to their prey'. These two edicts must have made the pirates and wreckers of the West Country rub their hands with glee: and when, from 1634 onwards, Charles I tried to levy Ship Money 'for the safety of the seas' against 'certain pirates . . . as well Turks, enemies of the Christian name, as others' (Spanish corsairs were in fact much more active along the south-west coast), the tax was resisted as one more example of royal tyranny.

The most spectacular Barbary raid was that on Iceland in 1627, when Reykjavik was plundered of salted fish, a quantity of hides, and four hundred – some accounts say eight hundred – men, women and

Captain Kidd's men burying the treasure he had to leave behind, as portrayed by Howard Pyle.

(Overleaf) A late-seventeenth-century painting of action between a Dutch fleet and Barbary pirate galleys.

144

1 Ottoman miniature of 1557 ows the true Kheir-ed-Din rbarossa, statesman and miral, received by Sultan leyman the Magnificent.

children. The pilot on this expedition was a Danish renegade, there were at least three English renegades in the corsair fleet, and it was commanded by a Dutchman, Jan Jansz (known as Murad Rais), the most colourful and best documented of all the Turk-turners except Ward and Danziker. Jansz, who plundered all Christian shipping (his sole tribute to national sentiment was to fly the standard of the Prince of Orange when attacking a Spaniard), had moved from Algiers to Sallee with a fleet of about eighteen sail that concentrated on East India and Guinea traders.

The port was nominally subject to the Emperor of Morocco, but shortly after Jansz's arrival in 1620 the Sallentines declared themselves independent and established a pirate republic governed by a committee of fourteen renegade captains. The Sallentine Republic was recognized and even courted by the European powers, and a Dutch consul, calling at Sallee in 1640, found Governor Murad Rais in the great hall of a heavily-fortified castle 'seated in great pomp on a carpet, with silk cushions and servants all around him'. When or how he died is not known, though his biographer, who calls himself 'a schoolmaster of Oostzaan' and professes to be greatly shocked by Jansz's desertion of his wife and family in Haarlem, concludes with the edifying but vague statement that 'his end was very bad'.

The strangest and most sinister pirate community in the Mediterranean was that of the Uskoks. Based at Segna, near Fiume, on the Adriatic, and protected by a labyrinth of creeks, the inhabitants of this region – unconquered by the Turks – had for centuries been notoriously tough and elusive brigands. Nominally subjects of the Habsburg Empire, they were commended as Christian warriors by the Pope (who bought galley-slaves from them) but spent most of their time attacking Venetian ships. They were on safe ground here, for the fact that the Venetians were fellow-Catholics did not prevent Italians and Spaniards from plundering them mercilessly. Theologians employed by the Viceroy of Naples to find pious excuses for this piracy denounced the Venetians as doubly-damned heretics: for not only did their vessels carry Muslim goods but (thanks largely to the activities of Neapolitan, Tuscan, and Uskok corsairs) many of those vessels were hired from English, German and Dutch infidels.

Never numbering more than five hundred active marauders, the Uskok fleets were joined by outlaws and adventurers from every port in Italy, including Venice. So long as they could find – or plant – a scrap of Muslim merchandise, they classified themselves as crusaders. A dozen or so shallow-draughted Uskok *fuste* (medium-sized galleys) packed with musketeers and swarming to the attack with drums beating and flags flying proved more than a match for the largest Venetian galleys. The *corso* was the only significant industry, and the Uskoks were popular throughout Dalmatia as purveyors of cut-price loot.

By the seventeenth century these Illyrian gangsters, who had spies

in the Venetian bureaucracy, had extended their operations as far as Brindisi and held commissions from the Viceroy of Naples and the Duke of Ossuna. Captured Uskoks were slaughtered to a man and their heads displayed as tropies of victory in St Mark's Square, but the ranks were soon filled. The Uskoks lived by a mystique of violence. In 1601 a Venetian spy reported seeing the assembled inhabitants of Segna crawling on their bare knees from the harbour to the many churches and chapels to give thanks for 'their uninterrupted robberies and murders'. Priests and friars (who not only benefited from piracy but often sailed with the pirates) whipped their charges into a tribal frenzy, constantly preaching the duty of crusade. Any able-bodied male who ignored their urging was branded as a coward, and those families who could boast the greatest number of men hanged or beheaded as pirates were the most honoured. Uskok women cold-shouldered husbands or sweethearts who would not go pirating, and after a brief display of extravagant grief took another mate within a few days of the death of a 'crusader'.

The rulers of Venice, who never quite overcame a feeling of contempt for their guttersnipe adversaries, consoled themselves with the belief that the Uskoks were in league with the Devil. It was said that their women were sorceresses who, by muttering incantations over fires kindled in dark grottoes, could make the wind blow from any direction they pleased. 'Certainly,' Nicolò Donà, brother of the Doge, told the Senate, 'I have seen clouds piling up over those mountains so suddenly and violently that it seemed the result of sorcery rather than of nature.'

Uskoks ('Scochi') attacking a merchantman: the ferocity of these 'crusaders' more than made up for any difference in size.

Beside the Uskoks, the corsairs of Malta and Barbary seem rather tame, though for at least two centuries after Lepanto they eked out a very businesslike pseudo-holy war. In the second half of the seventeenth century, threatened or actual bombardments of Algiers and Tunis led to a series of agreements whereby English, French and Dutch shipping was exempted from attack in return for the payment of a tribute in specie or naval stores. This reduced the number of Christian 'enemies', virtually ended long-range forays beyond the Straits of Gibraltar, and caused a heavy concentration on Catalan, Italian and Greek traders.

The Turkish sultans allowed the Barbary states a large degree of independence. There was a parallel between the corsairs on the western fringe of the Ottoman empire and the horsemen of Crim Tartary to the north, who were also semi-autonomous. 'The Sultan has two wings with which he flies very far,' wrote a Venetian historian, 'Barbary on the sea and Tartary on the land; both are insatiable birds of prey.' But though packed with janissaries the corsair ships did not do much fighting. A show of pugnacity – shouted threats, a clapping of hands, banging on the sides of the dhow-like, lateen-rigged *feluccas*, and what Defoe would have called 'vapouring' with scimitars – usually sufficed. Cannon, muskets and bows (used by Barbary corsairs until well on in the eighteenth century: thirty arrows could be loosed in the time required to load and discharge a firearm) were seldom fired.

In fact the corsairs were more likely to encounter violence back at base than at sea. By the seventeenth century the janissaries, mainly recruited in the Levant, were the real rulers of Algiers and Tunis, their elected leaders, known as beys or deys, being more powerful than the pashas or bashaws appointed from Constantinople. Palace revolutions were frequent, political history a monotonous tale of poisonings, stranglings, and janissary revolts. The corsair communities, led by their captains (*rais*), were in constant friction with military leaders who favoured more emphasis and expenditure on inland expeditions against troublesome tribes. The tension between *rais* and *aghas* (military officers) sometimes came close to civil war. In Algiers the solidly built residences of the *rais* were grouped in a kind of sailors' ghetto with their crews and tradesmen clustered near by like villagers round the walls of a medieval fortress.

In Malta everyone – Grand Master, Knights of St John, businessmen, priests, nuns, seamen and peasants – invested in the *corso*, and liked to think of it as a religious duty. Administered by the Knights, the industry was directed mainly at the North African coast and Ottoman trade routes in the eastern Mediterranean. Prisoners and ships were more important than cargoes (mostly wine, grain, fish and fruit for the Barbary men: the Maltese did rather better with spices, silks, jewels and concubines as well as rice, wheat and coffee). Slave-powered galleys formed the major components of the French, Italian, Papal and Turkish fleets until the eighteenth century.

Demand was brisk for Turkish oarsmen, much valued for their toughness and stamina (Negroes and even Iroquois Indians were tried but found to be much less satisfactory).

The *corso* was reckoned to be a lifetime profession, with short summer cruises and a long off-season. Maltese corsairs could winter comfortably in the Greek islands. Argentiera, one of their main bases in the Aegean, had a population of eight priests and some five hundred women who, as a French traveller put it, 'live purely on the work of Nature; so that all merchants and corsairs can choose a female companion according to his particular fancy'.

Many of the Barbary *rais* were renegades, but they were outranked – and closely watched – at sea by the *aghas* commanding the janissary detachments. Maltese captains were mainly French, with some Corsicans and Spaniards. On both sides, the corsairs were mere pawns in a complex political and commercial game in which little was left to chance or individual initiative. French, English and Dutch governments, all in treaty relationship with the Barbary states, allowed their subjects to use the Grand Master of the Knights of St John as a front man to issue 'crusading' licences. The French secretly financed the fitting out of corsair vessels, but insisted that the number of prizes should be strictly rationed: there was to be no such overkill as had marred operations in the distant and unruly Caribbean.

Heavily-armed French merchantmen, further protected by agreements with the beys and deys, grabbed an increasing proportion of the Mediterranean freight-carrying business – at high rates which Italian, Greek and even Turkish and Venetian shippers were glad to pay in the knowledge that their goods would arrive at their destinations. French, English and Dutch merchants sent agents to the prize markets of Algiers and Tunis, Malta and Leghorn, to buy up stolen goods on the cheap. Bale marks were deftly altered by squads of specialists so that they could not be identified by their owners. Small wonder that talk about organizing a joint naval expedition 'to obliterate the Barbary pirates' was just talk, part of an elaborate charade of 'concern' which helped to create an image of Algiers as the Black Hole of Barbary – 'the city that has bankrupted God'.

This was a gross distortion. The six Barnstaple 'captives' in Algiers were quite possibly having the time of their lives as 'sea-artists' on the corsair circuit, and would have laughed at the very idea of being ransomed. Slavery was seldom permanent, and its horrors were overstated by redemptionist organizations which played on racial and religious prejudices to raise funds. For merchants and corsair officers on either side, capture and ransom was a routine, almost ritual, affair. Prisoners were often exchanged or repatriated as part of a peace or tribute deal, and there were three different categories of 'slavery'. Christian captives were treated as prisoners of war. If they apostasized they could, with luck, rise to social and political eminence. Georgian and Circassian slaves brought in from

Some of the Christian adventurers, welcomed in the Barbary States for their knowledge of shipbuilding and navigation, who 'turned Turk' to further their careers.

the Levant could not be ransomed or repatriated: but they could earn money and buy a measure of freedom and social status. Lowest on the scale were the Negro slaves who were herded up on foot from Kano or Bornu. Like the Jewish entrepreneurs who grew rich as ransom-fixers and distributors of stolen cargoes, they were the butts of Christian and Muslim contempt.

Domestic slaves in wealthy Muslim households had an easy life and wielded far more influence than they could have dreamed of as free men in Christendom. The *bagnos*, or slave barracks, of Algiers and Tunis, huge, rambling places capable of accommodating two thousand slaves, offered plenty of opportunities for advancement to resourceful prisoners. The courtyards were surrounded by stalls, mostly taverns or eating-shops, run by slaves who paid a rent to the Turkish *concierge*. Soldiers, sailors, and even prominent citizens sat at the tables drinking, smoking, talking business. The *bagnos*, with their Catholic, Orthodox, and Protestant chapels and resident priests, were the great cosmopolitan social centres of the Barbary towns. Emanuel d'Aranda, a Spaniard who spent some time in one as a prisoner in the 1640s, found the atmosphere so lively and entertaining that he often returned there after his release. Among the inmates were seamen from Dunkirk, Hollanders who had sailed to the East Indies, Japan and China, Danes and Hamburgers who had been whale-hunting off Greenland, Frenchmen who could tell you about Canada, Spaniards with stories of Mexico and Peru. Algiers and Tunis at the height of their power and prestige were the most beguiling cities in the Mediterranean. In their jostling, flourishing underworlds European adventurers found a degree of social mobility unknown in their own countries, and a complete indifference about their pasts. So alluring were the prospects of turning Turk that the Commissaire de la Marine in Algiers warned the authorities in France to 'instruct captains not to let anyone ashore here; for the Provençals especially will don a turban as easily as a night cap'.

But the heyday was over, the *bagnos* half-emptied, and the corsair fleets of Malta and Barbary drastically reduced, by the 1730s. Treaty obligations, though sometimes broken by deys and beys desperate for money and under threat of assassination, were more strictly enforced by the navies of the maritime powers who, thanks to the 'pirates', had now got a firm hold on Mediterranean trade. The Grand Master, under even fiercer pressure to sustain the industry to which the Maltese economy was geared, tried to keep the round going by allowing corsairs to sail under his 'magisterial' flag (and later the flags of Spain, Tuscany, Monaco, and even Russia). When French disapproval closed the Levant to them, a circumventing formula was evolved: 'We wished to pursue our cruise in Barbary, but a gale-force wind from the north-west blew us into the Levant.' But the argument that 'corsair ships of the Religion provide French subjects with experience at sea and indeed captains of fame and valour have always graduated from this school to the service of France', though true, cut

(Opposite) *The maritime powers, who had a financial and political interest in the corsairs' activities, occasionally sent a squadron to make a show of force – as in this late-seventeenth-century punitive expedition against Algiers.*

less and less ice. By the 1750s Malta and Algiers between them had no more than twenty corsair ships on the job instead of about a hundred. Tunis and Algiers were reduced to declaring war on each other to avoid almost total stagnation. Long-suffering Greek shipowners – armed with 'passes' sold in large quantities and at considerable profit by French, English and Dutch consuls – actually began to win a few cases in the notoriously time- and money-consuming prize courts of Malta.

During the French Revolutionary and Napoleonic Wars of 1793–1815 both Malta and Barbary enjoyed something of a renaissance, taking advantage of the fact that the fleets of the naval powers were otherwise occupied. Napoleon's occupation of Malta in 1798, when he freed some two thousand Turkish and Moorish captives and abolished the *corso*, was succeeded by a profitable burst of privateering under British auspices. Rais Hamidou, one of the last and boldest of Algerine corsair captains, was fully aware of the opportunities for sea-scavenging when great powers fall out. 'Allah bless Napoleon,' he said, 'for so long as he is victorious we will not be bothered,' and, with his brother Hamidan, he relentlessly pillaged the shipping of Portugal, Sicily, Naples, Genoa, Hamburg, Holland, Denmark and Sweden.

'White slaves' brought ashore at Algiers, c. 1700 – perhaps to an easier life and a better career than they might have expected at home.

Merchantmen from the United States seemed an easy target, though in 1795 a non-aggression treaty was signed and the US government paid protection money until 1810. 'Can anyone believe', raged the American consul at Tunis, 'that this elevated brute, the Dey, has seven kings of Europe, two republics, and a continent tributary to him, when his whole naval force is not equal to two line of battleships?' In 1799 the tribute amounted to £50,000, twenty-eight guns, ten thousand cannon-balls, and large consignments of timber, cordage and gunpowder. Yet Rais Hamidou and other Barbary and Sallee corsairs (including Peter Lisle, a Scottish renegade in Tripoli known – like Jan Jansz – as Murad Rais) continued to prey on American ships, reckoning that the United States navy was almost non-existent and a very long way off. Public outcry forced Congress to send a naval expedition in 1803, but, like the English, French and Dutch expeditions of 1620, 1655 and 1683, it achieved very little, and ended in disaster when the *Philadelphia* ran aground off Tripoli and was captured with her entire crew. A second expedition in 1815, led by Stephen Decatur, was more successful. In a running fight with his squadron (which flew the English flag), Hamidou's ship (also flying English colours) was forced to surrender, and Hamidou killed. The American boarding party was surprised to find the janissaries, 'having exhibited their usual bravery, quietly seated on the deck smoking their long pipes with their accustomed gravity'.

Napoleon's defeat, rather than the victory of Decatur's squadron, spelt the beginning of the end for the Barbary corsairs. Imperialist ambition as much as humanitarian sentiment lay behind the Congress of Vienna's resolution that 'the suppression of African piracy and white slavery is universally felt to be a necessity'. Deprived of connivance and tribute, the Barbary men defended their way of life with surprising and quite unpiratical tenacity. An attempt by the Dey to round up foreigners in the regency of Algiers as hostages was followed by a massacre of Italians in a church at Bona. In August 1816 a powerful Anglo-Dutch fleet commanded by Lord Exmouth and Vice-Admiral Baron von Capellan bombarded Algiers into temporary submission, killing hundreds of people, releasing 1,600 slaves, and forcing the Dey to make a public apology to the British consul (Mr McDonell), who had been chained up – 'half naked' according to *The Times* – in a cell for condemned murderers.

The Dey was strangled, but his successor, Ali Khoja, continued the defiance. The American consul reported that when he and other foreign envoys paid their first official call on the new ruler, they were forced to pass a line of corpses before reaching his presence, 'where we found him magnificently dressed with a book in his hand as if our entrance disturbed him in his studies'. Ali Khoja, who behaved like the Turkish corsair chiefs of legend, seems to have combined a taste for white concubines with the satisfaction of a racial vendetta. The kidnapping of Rosa Ponsombio, a Sardinian girl, on the steps of the French consulate, threw Admiral Sir Sidney Smith, President of the

Anti-Pirate Association for the Redemption of Slaves in Barbary, into paroxysms of righteous indignation. Rosa, who was said to have thrown a note over the seraglio wall warning the British, Spanish and Dutch consuls to guard their womenfolk closely, remained a prisoner of vice until 1818, when the Dey died and the publication of the following alleged extract from his diary sent thrills of horror through Christian newspaper-readers' breasts: 'Mr McDonell's daughter, pretty and young, for my harem; the Spanish consul's daughter, who is ugly, to serve the favourite. I shall have the British consul's head cut off and kill the lot if they dare to complain.'

During one of the French punitive expeditions, the Algerines were alleged to have fired off forty-eight French residents, including the consul, at the blockading squadron.

In an unwitting act of germ warfare, the plague which killed the Monster of Barbary was carried to Europe in Algerine ships. The corsairs ventured out again, the *bagnos* contrived a simulacrum of their former vivacity. After a solemn debate at the Congress of Aix-la-Chapelle, an Anglo-French squadron appeared at Algiers in September 1819 to bombard the city – with a diplomatic mission. Honours were about even in the ensuing verbal warfare. Lectured on the need 'to abandon these piratical depredations for the pursuit of innocent commerce', the Bey of Algiers and the Dey of Tunis contrasted the sobriety and order of their cities with the debauchery and corruption of Tangier under English rule, and pointed out that Lord Exmouth and his Anglo-Saxon 'pirates' had caused more misery and shed more innocent blood in a few hours than the Barbary 'navies' had in nearly three centuries of mercifully conducted 'defence measures'.

American and European consuls on the Barbary Coast in the 1820s lived almost as dangerously as their counterparts in Latin America in the 1970s. But this backs-to-the-wall resistance could not last for ever. 'One must pull out the evil by the roots, by besieging the city of Algiers, the soul of piracy,' wrote the French consul-general in 1819. 'Once fallen into the hands of Europeans it would drag down in its wake the other Barbary states that still refuse to respect the rights of man.' Eleven years later his advice was taken. After a six-week campaign, a French army nearly forty thousand strong bombarded and occupied Algiers. But though Tunis and Tripoli came to heel, the Rif pirates of Morocco remained a problem for the next thirty years, surviving English and French punitive expeditions, evading patrols, and plundering merchantmen until the late 1860s.

The last years of the Malta-Barbary corsair sequence merged into the long Greek struggle for independence. The Greek corsairs took full advantage of the fact that public opinion in Europe, thanks partly to the propaganda of Lord Byron and other romantic liberals, had been persuaded to regard them as champions of democracy, classical culture and Christian civilization oppressed by reactionary and barbaric Turks. The eastern Mediterranean witnessed a petty piratical scrimmage more vicious than any since the days of the Cretan and Cilician freebooters. The Greek 'navy' was on a buccaneer basis and the provisional government, at one time headed by a notorious pirate, had no control over characters who, as even the most fervent Friends of Greece admitted, were 'ill qualified to perform the delicate task of examining ships and not over-nice in their manner of executing their duties'. Regular bases were established at Skiathos and around the fortress of Grabusa in Crete. British naval patrols were powerless against corsairs who fled nimbly from one to another of the Aegean islands. Shipping was attacked as far west as Malta, and Captain Hamilton of HMS *Cambrian* observed that 'it is not merely at sea, but wherever a vessel anchors that she is in danger of being plundered; even those that bring provisions for a Greek garrison are plundered'. Survivors of attacks told gruesome tales. Some had been flogged with knouts until they could scarcely crawl, others had been abandoned on remote and barren islands, and Turkish captives were murdered with revolting cruelty.

The British government, however, was more outraged by the fact that the capture of so many cargoes from Smyrna caused a currant famine in London. After the destruction of the Turkish navy in Navarino Bay on 20 October 1827 by a squadron of British, French and Russian warships, the Commander-in-Chief, Admiral Sir Edward Codrington, warned the Greek government: 'Your enemy's fleet exists no more. Take care of yours, for we will destroy it, if need be, to put a stop to a system of robbery on the high seas which would end in your exclusion from the law of nations.' And early in 1828 HMS *Isis* smashed the pirate stronghold at Grabusa, sinking or burning dozens of brigs, schooners, and melodiously-named *misticos*.

A lettre de marque
(privateering commission)
issued in 1745 by the Duc de
Penthièvre, Admiral of France.

In Malta and Segna everyone had a stake in the *corso*. More or less th
same was true of St Malo, Dunkirk, Nantes and La Rochelle, th
most prosperous centres of *la course*. The *armateurs* (privatee
promoters) of St Malo were among the richest and mo:
magnificently housed people in France. Their bishops, who investe
heavily in the trade, assured them that their profits were perfectl
justifiable, since they were incidental to the main business of ruinin
the enemies of the King, Dutch and English. It was the custom fc
corsair companies to attend a benedictory Mass before sailing, an
many shipowners left large legacies to the Church Militant i
gratitude for its prayers and moral support.

In the eighteenth century, during the long colonial struggle wit
England, corsair activity reached a new peak and the *armateur*
profits soared: but the first flush of revolutionary sentiment, nc
unmixed with a desire to neutralize the effects of British naval powe
brought criticism of behaviour which contradicted the dogma of th
Brotherhood of Man and was assumed to be an evil manifestation c
the old, reactionary régime. In May 1792, acting on a proposal b
Benjamin Franklin, the National Legislative Assembly in Par
debated the abolition of privateering and a guarantee of immunity fc
unarmed merchantmen. But in January 1793 the Convention, havin
declared war on England, proclaimed in equally high-flown terms th
need for a great surge of patriotic privateering in 'a war of iron again:
gold'. Cleansed of the 'vile nobility', France would be invincibl·
'When our country was ruled by despots she gave birth to corsai
like Jean Bart and Duguay-Trouin. What can she not do under th
rule of Equality? When free men fight they must do so with fury. Oι
Grenadiers capture batteries of artillery at the point of the bayone
We have seen our Hussars fight on horseback on the ramparts. Yo
Corsairs must board the enemy axe in hand and cut down tho:
proud islanders, the despots of the Ocean.'

It was decreed that any cargo destined for an enemy port could t
confiscated – a regrettable necessity made inevitable by Britis
tyranny and France's vocation to 're-establish in the world, side b
side with America, the sacred Rights of Man'. In 1803 'commerc
destroyers', who had hurried eagerly to the attack in the Channel, th
Atlantic, the Caribbean, the Pacific and the Indian Ocean, wer
formally recognized as naval auxiliaries. This was the great age of th
French corsairs. In three years to the end of 1795 they took more tha
two thousand prizes. Much of the Jamaica fleet was captured. A
expedition to Labrador ravaged the fisheries and sank eight

ĻOUIS JEAN-MARIE DE BOURBON, DUC DE PENTHIEVRE,

GOUVERNEUR ET LIEUTENANT-GENERAL *pour le Roy en fa Province de Bretagne*, AMIRAL DE FRANCE, A TOUS ceux qui ces prefentes Lettres verront, SALUT. Sçavoir faifons, Que Nous avons donné Congé & permiffion à
Maiftre & Capitaine d   nommé   du
port de   tonneaux ou environ, monté de   pieces de Canons & de   Pierriers,
eftant de prefent au Port de   de faire équipper en Guerre & Marchandife l
armer & munitionner de toutes chofes neceffaires, & le charger de telles marchandifes que bon lui femblera, pourvû qu'elles ne

rohibées ni défenduës, pour aller trafiquer
aifant, faire la guerre aux Ennemis de l'Eftat, à tous Corfaires, Pirates, gens fans aveu, & autres qui voudront empefcher la liberté du Com-
Sujets du Roy; les attaquer en quelques lieux & endroits qu'il les pourra rencontrer, les prendre & amener prifonniers avec leurs Vaiffeaux, Equi-
Marchandifes, & exercer fur eux toutes les voyes & actes permis & ufitez par les Loix de la Guerre; à la charge par ledit
de garder & faire garder par ceux de fon Equipage, durant fon voyage, les Ordonnances & Reglemens de la Marine fur les peines y con-
e porter pendant fon voyage les Pavillons & Enfeignes des Armes du Roy & les noftres; de faire enregistrer le prefent Congé au Greffe de l'Ami-
lus proche du lieu d'où il partira; y mettre un Rôlle figné & certifié de lui, contenant les armes, munitions, les noms, furnoms, naiffances & de-
hommes qui s'embarqueront. Et à fon retour qu'il fera dans l'un des Ports du Royaume qui lui fera le plus commode, & avant de rien décharger;
r fidel rapport pardevant les Officiers de l'Amirauté & non autres, de ce qu'il aura fait pendant fon voyage; déclarera s'il a ramené tous fes hom-
s'il ne les a ramenez, le lieu où il les aura laiffez; lequel rapport & verification d'icelui il envoiera au Secretaire general de la Marine, pour eftre fur
Nous ordonné ce que de raifon. Et en cas de prife en Guerre, fera faire des procedures pardevant les Officiers de l'Amirauté, conformément aux Or-
, lefquelles feront pareillement envoyées au Secretaire general de la Marine, avant que lefdites prifes puiffent eftre déchargées, pour fur icelles eftre par-
né ce qu'il appartiendra. PRIONS ET REQUERONS tous Rois; Princes, Potentats, Etats, Republiques, Amis, Alliez & Confederez de cette
, leurs Amiraux, Gouverneurs de leurs Provinces, Villes, Ports, Havres & Paffages, Capitaines, Chefs & Conducteurs de leurs Vaiffeaux & Equi-
autres leurs Officiers & Sujets qu'il appartiendra, de donner audit   toute affistance, paffages & retraite en leurs Ports,
it Vaiffeau, & ce qu'il aura pû conquerir, offrant de faire le femblable lorfque Nous en ferons par eux requis. MANDONS ET ORDONNONS aux
raux, Lieutenans-Generaux des Armées Navales, Chefs d'Efcadres, Capitaines de Vaiffeaux, & à tous autres Officiers de Marine qu'il appartiendra,
curement & librement paffer ledit   avec fondit Vaiffeau & Equipage, & tout ce qu'il aura pû conquerir pendant fon
vertu du prefent Congé, fans lui donner ni fouffrir lui eftre fait ou donné aucun trouble ni empefchement, mais au contraire tout le fecours, ayde;
affistance dont il aura befoin: & ne fervira le prefent Congé que pour un feul voyage. EN TEMOIN dequoy Nous avons figné ces Prefentes, & à
appofer le Sceau de nos Armes & contre-figner par le Secretaire general de la Marine. A
ois d   mil fept cent

L.J.M. de Bourbon

PAR SON ALTESSE SERENISSIME;

Donkerque

*(opposite) Jean Bart of
Dunkirk, the most celebrated
French corsair, crippled the
Dutch herring fleets and raided
the coast around Newcastle-on-
Tyne with his North Sea
squadron.*

*After a remarkable privateering
sequence René Duguay-Trouin,
born in St Malo – the* cité
corsaire *– was appointed naval
commander in Brest and died
full of honours in 1736.*

bankers. From Guadeloupe in the Leeward Islands Victor Hugues, a
Marseillais whose business in Port-au-Prince, French Hispaniola,
had been ruined by the Haitian slaves' revolt, unleashed a full-
blooded campaign which turned Pointe-à-Pitre, the Guadeloupan
capital, into a second Tortuga.

Hugues, an ambitious and ruthless adventurer, made a fortune out
of 'revolutionary' piracy. So did the shopkeepers of Pointe-à-Pitre
and a cosmopolitan squad of corsair captains. Antonio Fuët, a sailor
from Narbonne known as Captain Moëda (Moidore), became a figure
of legendary recklessness and flamboyance when he bombarded a
Portuguese prize with guns loaded with gold coins for lack of cannon-
balls and grapeshot. The story goes that after this memorable
engagement, the surgeons of Fuët's ship, the *Sans-Pareil*, worked
feverishly with their scalpels to recover some of the coins from the
bodies of the dead, the dying and the wounded.

On his own initiative, Hugues declared war on the United States, accusing the Americans of selling arms and ships to the British. 'The very name of America', he announced, 'inspires only scorn and horror here. The Americans have become the reactionary enemies of every ideal of liberty, after fooling the world with their Quaker play-acting. We shall have to remind this treacherous nation that but for us, who squandered our blood and our money to give them their independence, George Washington would have been hanged as a traitor.'

So effective was 'the Brigands' War' on American merchantmen (whose captains were forced to sign certificates stating that their cargoes were British property) that in July 1798 Congress retaliated by declaring war on France in American waters: which in effect meant war on Victor Hugues, the self-styled Robespierre of the Isles, who refused to obey the orders of the 'counter-revolutionary' Directory in Paris and considered declaring war on it too in the name of the true Revolution. Only the Dutch were exempted from the plundering of his captains – Antonio and Modesto Fuët, Pierre Gros, Peg-leg Langlois, Joseph Murphy, Petréas the Mulatto – and they profited hugely as receivers of the booty of Pointe-à-Pitre, which for a few years became one of the richest places in the Americas.*

Some French corsairs, like Jean-Jacques Fourmentin of Boulogne, who was credited with capturing at least a hundred British ships between 1793 and 1814, were made Legionaries of Honour: all were regarded as national heroes. In St Malo, streets, hotels, garages and restaurants are still named after Robert Surcouf, who for nearly ten years was the scourge of British shipping in the Indian Ocean. The East India Company offered a reward of two and a half million francs for his capture, and Surcouf was often in trouble with French colonial authorities for illegal slaving and refusing to hand over prize goods (he threw barrels of gold-dust into the sea at Port Louis, Mauritius, rather than give them to the Governor as the local representative of the Revolution). Having piled up a considerable fortune, Surcouf married the daughter of a rich *armateur* and adapted easily to St Malo business methods, cheating the customs, falsifying accounts, and taking more than his stipulated share of prize goods.

In Britain's American colonies, the cliques which had organized the Pirate Round and bought the loot of the New Providence men continued to profit from smuggling and privateering. Until the war of independence, French shipping was the main target. From 1776 to 1783, and again during the war of 1812–14, the prizes were British. The rebel navy consisted of thirteen mouldering frigates,

The exploits of French corsairs during the Revolutionary and Napoleonic Wars made them national heroes and offset the failure of the regular navy. Streets and hotels in St Malo are still named after Robert Surcouf (1773–1827).

---

*Victor Hugues, the son of a baker in Marseilles, has so far been ignored by historians of the French Revolution. There is no biography of him, but he is the central figure in Alejo Carpentier's magnificent historical novel, *Explosion in a Cathedral* (London, 1963), now available in paperback.

Paul Jones shooting a Sailor who had attempted to strike his colours during an engagement: a print of 1779.

whereas Britain already had more than a hundred naval vessels in American waters. The Continental Congress therefore sanctioned one of the largest and most effective corsair extravaganzas of modern times. Anything that would float was commissioned – merchantmen, pilot boats, ferries, whalers, longboats, fishing smacks. 'The people have gone mad a-privateering', wrote one observer: and in some areas, especially off Hàlifax and in the Gulf of St Lawrence, the concentration of corsairs was such that they sometimes attacked each other. Thanks to the hospitality of France, American or American-commissioned French privateers roamed from the Shetlands to Gibraltar.

Minor epics of daring were common. A Chesapeake barque cruising in the Irish Sea was so tiny that the captain of a prize mistook it for a pinnace and asked the crew where they had left their ship. John Paul, the seafaring son of a gardener on Lord Selkirk's estate near Kirkcudbright, changed his name to John Paul Jones and emerged as one of the most impudent of rebel 'pirates', raiding the coasts of England, Scotland and Ireland and sailing up the River Dee to loot Lord Selkirk's castle. His recklessnesss is celebrated in a ballad:

Our carpenter being frightened unto Paul Jones did say,
'Our ship she leaks water since fighting today.'
Paul Jones then made answer in the height of his pride,
'If we can't do no better we'll sink alongside.'

In many New England ports privateering was the principal business. Everyone invested in the corsair industry – including George Washington, who dined off china that had once belonged to the Solicitor-General of the British West Indies. Supply-ships to the British army were regularly intercepted, and the West India trade was disrupted by corsairs sailing from Martinique with French crews and French papers. Linen ships from Dublin had to sail under convoy, 10 per cent insurance was charged from Dover to Calais, in Portsmouth and Plymouth receipts from harbour dues were cut by half, the Liverpool trade fell off so steeply that ten thousand men were thrown out of work, and the *Annual Register* for 1778 reported that 'the Thames presented the unusual and melancholy spectacle of numbers of foreign ships, particularly French, taking in cargoes of English commodities for various parts of Europe'.

The 1812 war was also fought almost entirely by corsairs and to almost equally devastating effect – despite fears that the British navy could establish a blockade three or four vessels deep and still have a reserve. American shipwrights came up with a secret weapon in the form of the Baltimore clippers. Long, low in the water, with tall, raked masts and a glorious spire of canvas, they tormented British ships of the line as mercilessly as Hawkins's new-model ships had plagued the Spanish Armada. Once again, in the opening months scores of pilot boats armed with one or two small guns went into action. *The Times* reported that in the West Indies American privateers were 'so daring as even to cut vessels out of harbours and send raiding parties to carry off cattle from the plantations'.

New York alone fitted out 120 cruisers which brought in 275 prizes and destroyed many more. One crew came back with 300,000 dollars' worth of booty after dodging seventeen pursuers. Profits were so regular and handsome that the New York legislature passed an 'Act to encourage Privateering Associations'. In August 1814 the London *Morning Chronicle* commented that 'the whole coast of Ireland from Wexford round to Carrickfergus is virtually blockaded by a few petty fly-by-nights'. Despite the presence of three frigates and fourteen sloops in Irish waters, the insurance rate rose to nearly 15 per cent. At Halifax it was $35\frac{1}{2}$ per cent if you could insure at all. The *True-Blooded Yankee* accounted for twenty-seven vessels in thirty-seven days, and her crew realized three million dollars in prize money, including substantial government bounties (one half the estimated value of any armed vessel destroyed).

Jefferson, whose humanitarian ideals had been sadly battered, supported the 'burn, sink or destroy' bounty policy with some misgiving but not without a certain aggressive relish. 'Encourage these privateers to burn their prizes and let the public pay for them,' he wrote to Monroe. 'They will cheat us enormously. No matter, they will make the merchants of England feel and squeal and cry out for peace.' He was right on both counts. The corsairs did cheat, and in London, Liverpool and Glasgow merchants did meet to deplore the depredations of 'a horde of American cruisers' and urge an end to the war. As a last face-saving device, editorial writers and MPs attributed the success of the corsairs to the fact that they were of English descent and had 'the blood of Drake' in their veins.

The end of the French and American wars was followed by a sharp explosion of lawlessness. Tens of thousands of seamen were discharged from the British navy and faced with unemployment. Reports came from the Caribbean, the Atlantic, the Gulf of Guinea and the Arabian Sea of crews mutinying, killing their officers, electing their own leaders and turning pirate. The London reaches of the Thames were infested with robbers. Eight men in a cutter held up the *Lady Campbell*, an East Indiaman, at Greenwich and got away with two chests of coins.

The West Indies, which had been swarming with French, British, Spanish and American privateers for the best part of forty years, now swarmed with about ten thousand ex-privateers. Some found employment in the improvised navies of the rebellious Spanish colonies during their wars of liberation. Others entered the service of Spain. Many simply scavenged a living, encouraged by the connivance of the authorities in Cuba and Puerto Rico. Using small, swift brigantines, schooners and sloops similar to those of the

Lafitte and his crew clearing the decks of an Indiaman.'

(Overleaf) *The moonlit battle off Scarborough on 23 September 1779 between John Paul Jones in the* Bonhomme Richard *and the* Serapis, *a British man-of-war, is one of the best-known of all sea-fights.*

buccaneers, they produced a crop of pirate captains – Diabolito, Charles Gibbs and Benito de Soto were the most notorious – who revived on a miniature scale the Montbars-Lolonois tradition of ruthlessness. Perhaps they were conscious, like Ali Khoja, that time was running out and that restraint would serve no purpose.

Gibbs, a Rhode Islander, was one of the prime villains of *The Pirates' Own Book*. He had served with distinction on privateers during the 1812–14 war, and had no mind to join the ranks of the unemployed. Enlisting in an Argentinian privateer, he seized the ship and plundered in the Caribbean, offering the crews of his prizes a choice of joining his company or being killed, and sometimes, it was said, killing for the hell of it. But the cruise of the *Black Joke*, captained by a Spaniard, Benito de Soto, was the great pirate event of the time. Taken on as mate in the *Defensor de Pedro*, a Portuguese slaver which sailed from Buenos Aires in 1827, de Soto gained control while the captain was ashore, turned non-mutineers adrift in a small boat, renamed the ship the *Black Joke*, and lurked in the Atlantic. Within weeks he and his company captured the *Morning Star*, an East Indiaman, raping the wives and daughters of soldiers and officials coming home on furlough and leaving those passengers and seamen who had not been killed to drown in the hold as water seeped through holes bored in the hull.

Several more prizes were taken around the Azores, the crews massacred and the ships scuttled. Homeward-bound East Indiamen were ordered to collect at St Helena and sail in convoy. De Soto now put in to La Coruña, his birthplace, bought false papers, and made for Cadiz, where he hoped to dispose of his plunder. Driven on to the rocks near Cadiz by a storm, he and his men posed as honest merchantmen whose captain had been drowned. The wreck was on the point of being sold for salvage when some of the crew who had drunk, and talked, too much were arrested. De Soto escaped to Gibraltar, where he cut quite a dash in his blue frock coat, white trousers and white sombrero until a chambermaid, searching his baggage, found some incriminating evidence and he was arrested, tried and hanged.

Jean and Pierre Lafitte, two brothers from St Malo who became the bosses of a pirate-cum-smuggling centre on the island of Grande Terre near New Orleans, also exploited the confusion of the times. When the Governor of Louisiana offered a reward of five thousand dollars for the capture of Jean Lafitte dead or alive, Lafitte replied by posting an offer of fifty thousand dollars for the capture of the Governor. During the 1812 war he was offered a large bribe – and a commission in the Royal Navy – to fight on the British side, but, deciding that patriotism might be a better bet, offered the services of his gangsters to General Jackson in the siege of New Orleans. They defended the city so efficiently that Lafitte became something of a national hero and seems to have been rewarded by a tacit agreement not to interfere with his private enterprise. Combined operations by the US and British fleets put an end to this – and to the piratical free-for-all in the Caribbean – in 1823. Jean Lafitte was reported killed in an engagement with a British sloop-of-war. Some writers, however, claim that he did not die, but fled to Paris. There, it is said, he lived comfortably but did not lose an urge to set the cat among the pigeons: a whim which he satisfied by helping to finance publication of a swashbuckling manifesto by a talented literary corsair called Karl Marx.

The Gibbs-de Soto-Lafitte period is rich in pirate ballads. The tale of the *Flying Cloud*, a Guinea slave clipper that went on the account in the Caribbean, was based on a temperance booklet, *The Dying Declaration of Nicholas Fernandez*, purporting to be the confession of a member of de Soto's crew:

My name is Edward Hallahan, as you may understand,
I was born in the town of Waterford in Erin's happy land.
My parents raised me tenderly in the care of God likewise,
But little did I think I'd die 'neath Cuba's sunny skies. . . .

We've ravished and plundered many ships down on the Spanish Main,
Caused many a wife and orphan child in sorrow to complain,
We caused their crews to walk the plank, gave them a watery grave,
The saying of our captain was, 'A dead man tells no tales'.

Bold Manning tells of a Gibbs-like desperado who leads a massacre (and summarily settles a dispute) on a captured Liverpool trader:

These bold and crafty pirates,
With broadsword in hand,
They went on board of the merchant ship
And slaughtered every man . . .
They hunted the ship all over
And ransacked everything,
At last they found a female
In the after mess cabin.

Some did stomp and some did swear
They would make her their bride,
'Stand back, stand back!' says Manning,
'I'll soon put a stop to your strife!'
He boldly rushed upon her,
A brute without fear or dread,
Boldly rushed upon this female
And severed off her head.

In *The Bold Princess Royal*, there is great rejoicing when the merchantman outsails a 'close pirate' flying the black flag:

We shook out our close reefs, spread topgallantsails also,
With royals and skysails from the pirate we did go,
He chased us the whole day but could make no way,
He brailed in the spanker and then bore away.

Now all my brave boys, since the pirate has gone,
Here's a cask of good whiskey, another of rum,
Go down to your hammocks, boys, there drink till day,
For the bold *Princess Royal* from the pirates got away.

In Africa and Asia, European governments decided what was piracy and sent the navy to deal with it. This process had begun with the appearance of the Portuguese in eastern waters, but did not reach its pirate-imperialist climax until the Royal Navy, with occasional help from the United States (and in conjunction with adequately paid and therefore reasonably honest colonial officials), achieved on a global scale what Pompey had done in the Mediterranean eighteen centuries before.

The Pirate Coast is a case in point. For about two centuries the murderous rivalry between Portugal, Holland and England for control of the trade routes provided the only significant piracy in the Persian Gulf. In 1798 the Sultan of Muscat and Oman signed a treaty with Britain to exclude French and Dutch traders, but frequent civil wars made it impossible to fulfil the agreement. A fanatical and

Muscat harbour, beyond which lay the 150-mile stretch of the Persian Gulf known for centuries as the Pirate Coast.

xenophobic religious movement founded by Mohammed bin Abdul Wahab, who demanded all-out war on defilers of the Faith, had conquered Arabia, capturing Mecca and Medina and enlisting the aid of the seafaring coastal tribes. The Joasmis, Khalifahs and Jalahamahs pillaged as far east as Bombay, attacking East Indiamen and British warships. In 1804 some captured British officers and men were taken to the Joasmi capital, Ras-al-Khaima, and put on display as curiosities. It was reported that 'the Joasmi ladies were so minute in their enquiries that they were not satisfied without determining in what respect an uncircumcised infidel differed from a True Believer'.

In 1809 this and other outrages were revenged by a punitive expedition from Bombay consisting of two frigates, nine cruisers, a regiment and a half of regulars and a thousand Indian troops. Ras-al-Khaima was taken, looted and burned, sixty ships in the harbour destroyed. But in 1816 the Joasmis opened a campaign of plunder in the Red Sea. Sheikh Hassan of Ras-al-Khaima replied to a stiff note from Bombay that if his men were denied their ancient 'privilege' of robbing Indian vessels there would be nothing left for them to rob, and that in any case if he tried to prevent them he would be assassinated. For the next two years the *baggalas* and *batils* of the Arab corsairs, three-hundred-ton dhows with huge sails, towering poops, and elaborately-carved sterns, had a last tremendous fling. They tended to kill most of their captives because they considered it a cardinal sin to rob the living. In the West this quasi-ritual mass murder was taken to be the result of an insensate blood-lust.

To this day, in markets and coffee-shops along the Arabian coast, old men tell stories of Rahmah bin Jabr. J. S. Buckingham, British Resident at Bushire, who met Rahmah towards the end of fifty years of freebooting (a Jalahamah, he seldom attacked British ships since he hoped to get help from the Royal Navy in his feud with the Khalifahs), described him as 'having a meagre trunk, with four lank members, all of them cut and hacked and pierced with wounds from sabres, spears and bullets'. His face was 'naturally ferocious and ugly,

The British frigate Nereid
*engaging a fleet of Joasmi dhows,
. 1809.*

now rendered still more so by several scars and the loss of an eye. This Butcher Chief, who is said to have two hundred wives, affects great simplicity in garb and manners – to a degree which is disgusting. His usual dress is a shirt which is never taken off until it is worn out, no drawers or covering for the legs, a large black goat's skin wrapped over all, and a close-fitting handkerchief on his head.'

A blast of grape-shot had so shattered his left arm that the elbow was connected to the shoulder by withered skin and tendons stiffened with silver wiring. When asked if he could still despatch an enemy with his boneless arm, Rahmah supported his elbow with his right hand, grasped a dagger in his left, and 'drew it back and forth, saying that he could still slit a few throats'. Captain Loch of HMS *Eden*, who talked with Rahmah in 1819, remarked that his small stature, stooping, waddling gait and bonnet-shaped hood 'gave him the appearance of a hellish sorceress'. Yet when he walked in the streets 'he was gazed at by all and followed by a crowd of children'.

175

Joasmi resistance was broken in 1819 by a powerful naval squadron, which, with some East India Company cruisers and the fleet of the Sultan of Muscat, bombarded strong points along the Pirate Coast up to the islands of Bahrain, and landed a mixed force of seven thousand British, Indian and Arab troops to complete the work of destruction. Though warned by Captain Loch that he must stop his piracy, since most ships carried British or British-Indian property even if they did not fly the British flag, Rahmah went on plundering from his base at Katif with Arab, Negro and Baluchi crews. Seventy years old and blind, he put to sea (or, in an Arab historian's phrase, 'took the garments off the forearm of endeavour') for the last time in 1826 with one ship, the *Ghatrusha*, to do battle with the fleet of his Khalifah rival, Sheikh Suleiman of Bahrein. The *Ghatrusha* was rammed by a *baggala* captained by Suleiman's son, Sheikh Ahmed. On the high poop, Rahmah's favourite slave gave him a running commentary on the terrible combat – blood streaming over the decks and staining the sea, the enemy gaining ground. As the last of his bodyguard fell, Rahmah snatched a firebrand and hurled it into the powder magazine, killing himself, his eight-year-old son, and many of the Khalifahs, including Ahmed. The spectacular exit which European pirates, in their cups, sometimes boasted they would make had finally been made by a Wahabi teetotaller intoxicated with pride and hatred.

During the first decade of the nineteenth century the waters around Canton, Macao and Hongkong were thick with pirate junks, but it was piracy with a revolutionary tinge. Privateer crews back from a war with Annam joined forces with hordes of impoverished fishermen and dock workers to wage war on corrupt Mandarin rule, and helped to pay for it by plundering European shipping. By 1807 Ching Yih, who had rejected an attempt to buy him off (he was offered the Mastership of the Imperial Stables), commanded a fleet of six hundred war-junks. When he was drowned his widow, Ching Yih Saou, expanded the force until it comprised eight hundred large junks and nearly a thousand smaller ones, divided into six squadrons crewed by seventy thousand men – and women. Sailors were allowed to have their wives on board, and by all accounts they were almost as effective as the men.

Captured crews were given the choice of joining the pirates or dying very painfully. Richard Glasspoole, an officer on an East Indiaman captured in Canton River in 1809, witnessed a scene of forcible recruitment. 'Those who refused to comply had their hands tied behind their backs, a rope from the mast-head rove through their arms, and were hoisted a few feet from the deck. Six men flogged them with twisted rattans until they were apparently dead; then hoisted them to the mast-head, left them hanging nearly an hour, then lowered them and repeated the punishment until they died or obeyed.'

The boats of HMS Dido, *a ship of the China Squadron, in action against a native river stronghold in Borneo.*

The Chinese pirates' articles resembled those of Bartholomew Roberts in their vetoes on desertion ('if any man goes ashore without permission he shall have his ears perforated, and repeating the offence he shall suffer death'), pilfering, and sexual licence ('no person shall debauch at his pleasure captive women: he must first ask the quartermaster for permission and then go aside in the hold. To use violence against any woman shall be punished by death'); but Ching Yih Saou herself is said to have taken a whole series of lovers. Ultimately she and most of her lieutenants bought an imperial pardon and directed a large smuggling combine.

The pirates who continued to hover off Hongkong did not meet any serious opposition until the China Squadron set about the task of pacification in the 1840s, largely as a result of the British government's determination to thwart the Emperor's efforts to control the opium trade. India was the largest producer of opium and China was the main market for it. Hence the Opium Wars and the 'cession' of Hongkong, classic examples of buccaneering free trade. Raids on the opium clippers were seen by many Chinese as acts of patriotism, and one corsair captain, Shap-ng-Tsai, was given mandarin rank in 1849 after his fleet had been defeated in battle with the China Squadron. War junks, with their inflammable bamboo matting sails and minimal firepower – they relied on ramming and boarding – were sitting targets for naval broadsides. Within a few weeks nearly a hundred junks were destroyed and some two thousand pirates killed without a single British casualty. Hongkong merchants presented Captain John Hay and his victorious officers with a service of plate apiece, and the Treasury paid out more than £40,000 in bounties at £20 for every pirate killed or captured.

The process of pacification was now extended to other native obstructors of progress. The pirates of the Malay Archipelago, in their magnificent *prahus*, rowed by slaves and manned by warriors in coats of mail and scarlet-plumed helmets, were doomed to similar retribution. Often they formed the predatory navies of a multitude of sultans and rajahs. Like Chinese, Japanese and Indian corsairs they had in the past made temporary alliances with European interlopers, but by the early nineteenth century, when these were threatening to disrupt the time-honoured cycle of slave raids and ransom snatches, they tried belatedly to combine against the common enemy. For nearly twenty years, until the US frigate *Potomac* landed a force of marines on the Sumatran coast to burn his ships and wreck his stronghold at Kuala Batu, Raga, the 'Prince of Pirates', waged a highly successful war on European shipping in the Straits of Macassar, capturing about fifty vessels and – in accordance with a vow of racial revenge – enslaving or killing their crews (he was said to take special pleasure in personally beheading English officers).

An English visitor to the bazaar at Kuala Batu helped to whip up jingo sentiment with a scandalizing report that the articles on sale included Bibles, European women's underwear, and European prostitutes. James Brooke, the self-made White Rajah of Sarawak, was soon complaining of 'formidable piratical hordes' (they included Dyak tribesmen who combined conventional plunder with head-hunting) who were 'allowed to commit with impunity the most dreadful outrages, there being no naval force to keep them in check'. In 1843 he and Captain Sir Henry Keppel met at Singapore to plan their campaign. They concluded that 'the only way to strike at the root of the evil would be to destroy the piratical strongholds in the interior of Borneo'. In the next six years hundreds of loot-seeking native *prahus* rowed upriver to join in the fun behind the gunboats.

The campaign was climaxed in 1849 by a grand assault on the Dyak stronghold at Batang Maru on the River Saribas. The expeditionary force, led by Brooke in his own *prahu*, the *Singh Rajah* ('Lion King'), included the East India Company's steamship *Nemesis*. Dyak *prahus*, racing to the attack, were smashed in dozens by accurate gunfire, and the *Nemesis* caused havoc with her flailing paddle-wheels. When Commander Farquhar, who himself received a cool £2,757 for a few hours' work, claimed a £20,700 bounty (for five hundred pirates killed or captured and 2,140 'dispersed'), the anti-imperialist lobby in the Commons protested that this was a shocking waste of public funds. Such rewards, they argued, were ludicrously disproportionate to the risks involved. Was not this kind of head-hunting more reprehensible than that of an honest, if benighted, Dyak? And why should men who slaughtered tribesmen armed with bows, spears, swords and blow-pipes be paid four times as much as those who

Dyak tribesmen of Sarawak – head-hunters and pirates – performing a war-dance.

gained a hard-won victory against a European enemy? If the figures were accurate they told a tale of wanton butchery: if they were not they were evidence of a corrupt mentality which pandered to the blood-lust of the ignorant masses in the pursuit of private gain. It was even suggested that many of the Dyaks were peaceful traders, commercial rivals whom Brooke found it convenient to kill off. In China and Borneo, the Little Englanders maintained, naval police forces were 'more dreaded than any of the pirates they hunted so implacably'. Four years later a Royal Commission reproved Brooke – for 'unseemly behaviour' in allying himself with savages.

The West Africa Squadron's anti-slaver blockade was perhaps inspired as much by economic considerations (West Indian sugar production had been cut back since it was cheaper to buy from Brazil) as by William Wilberforce and other emancipationist paladins: but it was a tough and comparatively noble chore. Slavery was abolished throughout the British Empire in 1834, and the slave trade classified as piracy; but the demand for slaves in the southern states of America, Brazil, Cuba and the Arab world (an African bought on the Gold Coast for £1.50 could be sold in Brazil for £125) made sure that the suppression of these pirates would be a much more formidable task than the obliteration of Kuala Batu and Batang Maru.

Slave clippers were easily identified by the stench of their cargoes and the sharks hovering in their wake. When caught they were burned or sawn in half at Destruction Bay, Sierra Leone. Sometimes a chase lasted for several days, since the clippers were built for speed. Palmerston's 'darling policy' was bitterly criticized by frustrated businessmen in Liverpool and Bristol, who sneered at the work of the 'sentimental squadron'. Recruitment was not easy. Malaria and gut-rotting African liquor took a heavy toll, and the government paid out nearly £2 million in hard-earned prize money to keep the Squadron up to strength. Even so, the 150,000 slaves rescued by the Royal Navy *en route* for the Americas between 1810 and 1864 represented at most ten per cent of the total number exported. The victory of the North in the American Civil War subtracted one great market; but not until the scramble for Africa got going in earnest and other imperialist powers, reckoning that cheap labour should be kept *in situ*, reinforced the British patrols, did the blockade become really effective.

In the meantime, blockade-running produced some highly re-sourceful characters. Philip Drake, an American, changed his name to Don Felipe Drax and masqueraded as a Brazilian after the British slave-trade ended. In *Revelations of a Slave Smuggler*, published in 1860, he claimed to have shipped more than seventy thousand slaves in five years, and remarked that 'business is getting better every year. If you should hang all the Yankee merchants engaged in it, others would soon take their places.' Profits were at least as fat as they had been at the height of the Pirate Round. Drake owned an island in the Gulf of Mexico on which he kept up to two thousand Negroes ready for sale to dealers from Havana, New York and Rio de Janeiro. Two years after the publication of his book, a US law of 1808 defining the importation of slaves as piracy was at last enforced. The scapegoat was Nathaniel Gordon of Portland, Maine, captured with a cargo of nearly a thousand Negroes by the *Mohican*, an American patrol ship. Gordon's trial in New York for piracy was a sensational event. 'Citizens, come to the rescue!' urged posters. 'Shall a judicial murder be committed in your midst? Captain Gordon is sentenced to be executed for a crime which has virtually been a dead letter for forty

Although piracy was virtually
dead by the end of the nineteenth
century, the popular tradition
survives: Robert Newton as
Long John Silver in the 1950
Walt Disney production of
Treasure Island.

years.' The Tombs Prison was surrounded by armed marines when
Gordon was hanged there on 8 March 1862, the last white man to
suffer death as a pirate.

In the Niger Delta African pirates, headed by one Abokko, who
called himself Superintendent of River Traffic, launched their own
Raga-like challenge to the white invaders. They took a number of
prizes, notably Samuel Crowther (the first African Bishop appointed
by the Anglican Church Missionary Society), for whom Abokko
demanded a ransom of a thousand bags of cowrie shells and coral
beads. Gunboats soon dealt with this kind of disorder, and finally put
paid to a wily opponent on the Congo, where for five years Manuel
Vacca, a Portuguese and former slave-trader, controlled a fleet of
African 'privateers' from a series of jungle hideouts. In 1875 Vacca's
braves looted and burned the *Geraldine*, a British schooner stuck on a
sandbank, and Commodore Hewett of the West Africa Squadron led
an expedition of 250 sailors and marines briefed 'to inflict such
punishment that the outrage will not be repeated'. Forty villages
were burned, hundreds of canoes destroyed, palm and banana
plantations cut down. The pacification of the Congo Delta was
completed by a solemn palaver with eight tribal chiefs conducted to
the accompaniment of martial airs played by a Royal Marine band.

The decline of piracy has been variously attributed to the abolition
of privateering and the slave trade, the evangelization of the masses,
the tax on gin, the industrial revolution (steel-and-steam ships),
penal and social reform (including better pay and conditions in the
navy and merchant marine), increasingly effective centralized
government, and telegraphic communications.

Pirates had been pioneers of improved marine technology in the
age of sail. Their intelligence service was usually better than that of
the fumbling forces of the state, and like land brigands they were
often shrewd businessmen, keen students of the law of supply and
demand moving warily in the shifting, shrinking *terrain vague* where
loot was translated into cash and vital supplies. Privateering and
piracy had always gone together, offering sometimes considerable
rewards at less risk than most citizens ran from sudden death by
poverty, disease, or judicial murder ashore. But by 1815 the British
navy, a match for all other sea forces combined, had no further call for
auxiliaries, while professionalization of the naval service and large-
scale construction of specially designed warships made the use of
converted merchantmen less and less practicable. During the Crim-
ean War both sides renounced the commissioning of privateers – an
easy sacrifice since Russia had none to commission and the British
and French did not need any. At the Paris Peace Conference of 1856
Britain, France and Russia solemnly abolished privateering, an
example soon followed by the United States and most other
countries.

(Overleaf) A scene on board a
slave clipper. In 1834 Britain
defined slave-trading as piracy
and maintained naval patrols
along the West African coast,
but during the next thirty years
hundreds of thousands of
Africans were shipped through
the blockade.

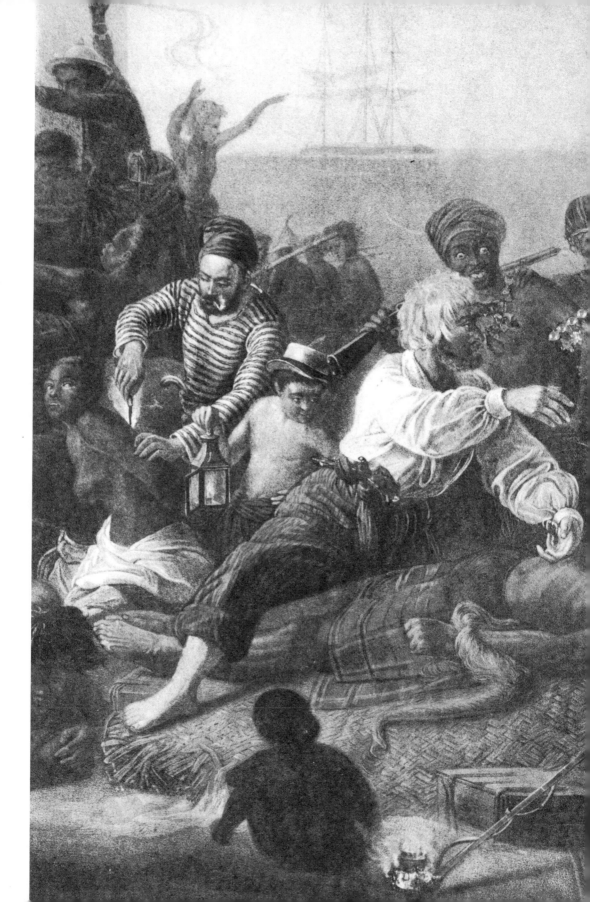

Faced by ever more efficient police action, piracy faded out everywhere as the risks became too great or the returns too small. Unrestricted submarine warfare as practised by Germany in two world wars was denounced as a revival of piracy; but it was much closer to the commerce-destroying tactics of French and United States privateers during the British naval blockade of 1793–1814, and its bleak push-button technique lacked a whole dimension of excitement and sensual gratification. The Chinese hijackers of the 1920s and 1930s, daring as they were, do not qualify as pirates, being gangsters only briefly afloat and in some cases students with a Marxist grudge against Western imperialism and luxury passengers. Perhaps the last seafaring gangsters in the pirate tradition were Eli Boggs, Bully Hayes and Ben Pease.

Boggs, an American, eluded the policemen of the China Station for years, having supervised the construction of a fleet of pirate junks with hulls of rakish design modelled on those of the opium clippers he plundered. He was said to have cut up a rich Chinese merchant and sent the pieces ashore in a bucket, warning that, if a large ransom were not paid immediately, the mandarins he still held prisoner would be similarly treated. His cruelty and cunning were favourite topics of conversation in the bars and billiard-rooms of Hongkong in the 1850s, and his capture in 1857 was dramatic enough to make headlines all over the world. Boarding-parties in two cutters were almost blown out of the water when his junk exploded minutes after Boggs had dived overboard and struck out for the shore. Overtaken by a more powerful swimmer, he trod water and, stabbing at his pursuer with a knife, was knocked out with a right swing to the jaw. The *Times* correspondent at his trial reported that 'it was almost impossible to believe that this handsome boy with carefully brushed hair, girlish face, charming smile, and delicate hands could be the man whose name had been associated with the boldest and bloodiest acts of piracy'.

During the 1920s and 1930s Chinese hijack gangs brought off a number of daring captures at sea – these men, under guard on a British warship, were some of the unlucky ones.

The hero who knocked out the dandy renegade was Captain Henry ('Bully') Hayes, the skipper of an American trading barque of dubious reputation. He not only received a reward of a thousand dollars for his bravery, but made off with two chests of silver specie from one of Boggs's junks. Himself a man of considerable charm and a noted bar-room raconteur (he had worked in New Zealand as a member of a travelling minstrel group), he used the money to launch himself and a small group of beachcombers on a career of gun-running, black-birding (kidnapping natives, who were sold as plantation slaves) and robbing isolated trading posts in the South Sea Islands. He survived precariously and nefariously in company with Ben Pease, Paunchy Bill and Paddy Coney (the sort of characters Stevenson wrote about in *The Ebb Tide*), until the missionaries and the Royal Navy combined to clear the Pacific of this 'buccaneer scum' in the 1870s.

Hayes and Pease, the latter famed for his advice 'never to take more

than two wives on a voyage and choose 'em with care', several times helped each other out of tight corners. Having impressed the British consul at Samoa with a twenty-one-gun salute on Queen Victoria's birthday, and staged a violent public quarrel with Hayes – then under mild detention awaiting transport to Australia to stand trial for piracy – Pease spirited the prisoner away. Five years later Hayes, in gaol at Manila, spent his time studying devotional tracts and so impressed the bishop with his piety that he was not only received into the Church but unconditionally released. Soon afterwards he was murdered by a Scandinavian mate who broke his skull with an iron bar and threw his body into the sea. There he floats still in the mind's eye, a drifter, a rover, a rogue, a man wedded to the sea as the element of plunder and, in the end, inseparable from it, whatever his dealings ashore: a pirate.

Chapter Ten **An Alternative Society?**

Privateering and elaborately organized pirate syndicates had proved
capable of enlisting the enthusiasm and energy of whole communities. How far did pirates proper – the few who by inclination or
necessity cut as loose as possible from 'civilization' – succeed in
creating an alternative society? Did any such idea even enter their
heads?

The only recorded instance – seized on by a host of writers
unwilling to look a myth horse in the mouth – is that of Captain
Misson. We are told that this noble soul, revolted by the greed and
injustice of the world, and dreadfully disillusioned by a visit to Rome
the corrupt headquarters of his Faith, took to piracy in the spirit of a
moral crusader. Misson and his mentor Caraccioli, a former Italian
monk turned garrulous Apostle of Reason, are said to have persuaded
the crew of the *Victoire* to strike a blow for human brotherhood and
enlightenment after the captain and other officers had been killed
during an engagement with the *Winchester*, an English man-of-war
off Martinique in the early 1690s. According to the chronicler, since
they were 'no pirates, but men resolved to affect the Liberty which
God and Nature gave them', a proposal by the boatswain to run up
the black flag and get down to business was vetoed after a series of
impassioned harangues, and amid cries of 'Long live the brave
Captain Misson and the noble Lieutenant Caraccioli!' it was agreed
to fly a white flag with the motto 'For God and Liberty' embroidered
upon it.

Prizes had to be taken to raise funds for the millennium, and we
learn that Caraccioli lost a leg in a fight with a Portuguese carrack off
Zanzibar. But courtesy and restraint were observed at all times. The
captain of an English ship from which some provisions were removed
praised the 'gentleness and candour' of his robbers and gave them
'three rousing cheers' as they sailed away. Negroes on a Dutch slaver
boarded in the Gulf of Guinea were freed and dressed in the clothes
of their oppressors – because, explained Misson, 'though distin-
guished from the Europeans by their colour, customs and religious
rites, they are the work of the same Omnipotent Being and endued
with equal Reason. We have not asserted our own Liberty to enslave
others.'

Proceeding to the isle of Johanna, Misson and Caraccioli practised
the racial equality they preached by marrying the daughters of two
native chiefs, and retired, with as many of the crew as wished to
accompany them, to Madagascar. There they founded Libertalia, a
brotherhood of the coast which, it was hoped, would set an example

of true Fraternity and give the missionary pirates 'some place to call their own, and a receptacle, when age or wounds had rendered them incapable of hardship, where they might enjoy the fruits of their labour and go to their graves in peace'.

It was decided that property should be held in common and funds, deposited in a central treasury, allocated according to need. Two ships, the *Childhood* and the *Liberty*, sailed round the island to chart the coasts and teach liberated slaves and native recruits the elements of seamanship. A Session House was constructed and at the first meeting Misson was elected Lord Conservator for a three-year term with Caraccioli as his deputy. Members of the Council were chosen for their ability without consideration of race or creed, and several Pirate Round companies are said to have opted in to Libertalia, notably that of Thomas Tew, who was elected Admiral of the combined fleet. The language difficulty was overcome by the invention of a lingua franca with elements of French, English, Portuguese and Dutch; and Misson gave the name of Liberi to his people, 'desiring in that might be drowned the distinctions of French, English, Dutch, African etc'.

Quarrels between men of different nationalities and companies nevertheless plagued the infant utopia, forcing Misson to acknowledge the need for discipline and a definition of property rights. But as laws multiplied, litigation increased and fraternity withered. Emergency sessions and moral sermons failed to prevent a deplorable tendency to build private empires and exploit the natives. This in turn provoked a Negro revolt which ended, we are told, in the massacre of most of the Liberi, while Misson and a handful of refugees who had escaped with him perished when their ship sank in a hurricane.

Libertalia (it is hardly necessary to add) never existed except in the mind of its inventor, Defoe, and, it may be, as a pipe-dream in the minds of some of the ex-pirates he met in Wapping and Rotherhithe. The long chapter on Misson in the *General History* not only lacks psychological credibility, like nearly all utopian propaganda, but is full of discrepancies. Protestant bias is apparent in the anti-papist origin of Misson's conversion. Defoe claims that 'we can be somewhat particular in the life of this gentleman, because by a very great accident we have got into our hands a French ms in which he himself gives a detail of his action', but covers his tracks by saying that Misson concealed the true name of his father, 'the master of a plentiful fortune in Provence'. The black jack was not being flown in the early 1690s, and Baldridge's journal – which makes no mention of Misson – and other sources show that although Tew's quartermaster and twenty-five other pirates stayed behind in Madagascar, Tew did not, but left St Mary's in December 1693 and arrived at Rhode Island a few months later with '£100,000 in gold and silver and a good parcel of elephant's teeth, bought up by the merchants of Boston'.

In his fantasy of Libertalia, Defoe may have been putting his tongue in his cheek or his heart on his sleeve – probably a bit of both; but by comparison with the priggish rhetoric of Misson and Caraccioli, Captain Bellamy's outburst – 'Had you not better make one of us than sneak after the arses of those villains for employment?' – rings refreshingly true, or at least likely: and in other chapters Defoe gives a far more convincing account of pirate settlements in Madagascar. He mentions that Captain Halsey, dying there of a fever, was buried after a salute of minute guns 'as many as he was years old, *viz* 46', and that his grave was 'set in a garden of water melons, fenced in with palisades to prevent his being rooted up by wild hogs'. Many other pirates died of malaria, venereal disease, and heavy drinking. Some were murdered by the natives or perished in the tribal wars which, to enlarge their 'kingdoms', they fomented. Those who escaped these hazards 'lived in a great deal of dirty state and royalty', marrying 'the most beautiful of the Negro women; not one or two but as many as they liked'. Their dwellings, 'rather citadels than houses', were camouflaged huts deep in the jungle surrounded by earthworks and approached by a narrow, maze-like path along which large thorns were 'struck into the ground with their points uppermost' to discourage night visitors. Thus 'tyrant-like they lived, fearing and feared by all': a state of affairs which helps to explain why so many preferred to return to their own countries and risk hanging.

Clement Downing, who sailed with Commodore Matthews on the pirate-hunting cruise of 1722, described in his journal a meeting with John Plantain, the self-styled King of Ranter (Antogil) Bay – one of the longest livers who took all. Born of English parents in Chocolate Hole, Jamaica, Plantain claimed to have turned pirate with the intention of getting together enough capital to set up in honest trade (after accepting a pardon). But after sailing with Condent, England and Taylor on three of the most lucrative cruises in pirate history, he had decided to stay in Madagascar, thinking it wise to lie low for a while, especially when he heard about Bartholomew Roberts's provocative exploits in the Caribbean.

An attempt to arrest Plantain, who appeared in a soiled courtier's suit with two pistols stuck in his sash, was foiled by a bodyguard of brawny and well-armed Negroes. The pirate king lived in a stockaded fortress with two other ex-rovers, a Scotsman and a Dane, and 'had many wives whom he kept in great subjection, and after the English manner called them Moll, Kate, Sue and Peg. . . . They were dressed in the richest silks and some of them had diamond necklaces.' After bartering gold and diamonds for hats, shoes, cloth and arrack, Plantain ran up the flag of St George and treated Matthews and his officers to a lavish feast. With much pride he showed off his favourite wife, Holy Eleanora Brown, the half-caste daughter of a rival pirate king killed in battle. She could recite the Lord's Prayer, the Creed, and the Ten Commandments, and had been rewarded for this accomplishment with a shower of jewels and twenty domestic slaves.

Downing relates that Captain England, now very near to a death 'occasioned by severe stings of conscience for his wicked course of life – a thing that seldom happens to this sort of men', was a pensioner on the bounty of Plantain, who, having murdered all his rivals, 'grew weary of his kingship and resolved to quit his territories'. He sailed, says Downing, to the Malabar Coast in a sloop with Eleanora Brown, and offered his services to Tulaji Angria, the pirate king of those parts – 'who, when he realized what course of life Plantain had followed and what a valiant fighting man he was, entertained him in a magnificent manner'.

Pirate cynicism is well hit off by Defoe in his account of Captain Anstis and his company, who, after taking French leave of Roberts's squadron in the Gulf of Guinea, crossed the Atlantic and established themselves on a small, uninhabited island in the Caribbean. Having despatched a fulsome petition to 'His Sacred Majesty King George ... that we, lying under the ignominious name and denomination of Pirates, may return to our native country and serve the nation to which we belong without fear of prosecution by the injured whose estates have suffered by the said Bartholomew Roberts and his accomplices during our forcible detainment by the said Roberts', they whiled away the months of waiting for a reply with such community games as 'dancing and other diversions agreeable to those sort of folks; and among the rest they appointed a mock Court to try one another for piracy, and he that was a criminal one day was made a judge another'. Defoe claims to have 'had an account of one of these merry trials. . . . The Court and criminals being appointed, as also counsel to plead, the judge got up in a tree and had a dirty tarpaulin hung over his shoulders by way of a robe, with a thrum' (coarse tarred yarn) 'cap on his head and a large pair of spectacles on his nose. . . . Below was an abundance of officers with crows, handspikes etc instead of wands, tipstaffs and suchlike. The criminals were brought out, making a thousand sour faces; and one who acted as Attorney-General opened the charge against them.'

The proceedings 'went something as follows':

Attorney-General : An't please your Lordship and you gentlemen of the jury, here is a fellow that is a sad dog, a sad, sad dog; and I humbly hope your Lordship will order him to be hanged out of the way immediately. He has committed piracy upon the high seas . . . and went on robbing and ravishing man, woman and child, plundering cargoes fore and aft, burning and sinking as if the Devil had been in him. . . . I should have spoke much finer than I do now, but that as your Lordship knows, our rum is all out and how should a man speak good law that has not drunk a dram?

Judge : Hearkee me, Sirrah, you lousy, pitiful, ill-looked dog; what have you to say why you should not be tucked up immediately and set a-sun-drying like a scarecrow?

Prisoner : An't please your worship's honour, my lord, I am as honest a poor fellow as ever went between stem and stern of a ship. . . . But I was taken by one George Bradley (the name of him that sat as Judge), a notorious Pirate, a sad rogue as ever was unhanged, and he forced me, an't please your honour . . .

West Africa, too, had some roystering pirate enclaves. Bartholomew Roberts, who seized two French patrol ships off Senegal and took them to Sierra Leone for conversion, found it a very congenial place, with a small community of traders – 'men who in some part of their lives have either been privateering, buccaneering or pirating . . . and still love the riots and humours of that sort of life. They live very friendly with the natives and have many of both sexes to be their *gromettas* or servants. The men are faithful, the women so obedient that they are very ready to prostitute themselves to whomsoever their masters shall command them.' The traders did business with English merchantmen, especially from Bristol, bartering slaves and ivory for beer, cider, wine, brandy and rum, so that 'there was what they call good living'. Notable characters, says Defoe, were Benjamin Gun of Rio Pungo and Captain Crackers, an ex-buccaneer 'who keeps the best house in the place, has two or three guns with which he salutes the pirates when they put in, and lives a jovial life with them while they are there'.

But perhaps the best description of a pirate community was given by William Dampier. In 1675 he sailed from Port Royal in a ketch going to trade sugar and rum for logwood at the camps on the Mosquito Coast where about 250 Englishmen, mostly buccaneers, made a hard living. Dampier was so taken with the free-and-easy comradeship of the camp at One Bush Key, on Terminus Lagoon near the island of Trist, that he went back there to set up in trade himself.

The cutters were grouped in companies of four to twelve men, living in tents or thatched huts. Negresses or Indian women cooked their food on barbecues – usually 'pork and pease or beef and dumplings'. Some had white wives bought in Jamaica for £30 apiece. They slept in hammocks and fashioned chairs and benches from logs and planks. Felling and hauling in mangrove swamps under a hot sun was gruelling work, and it was followed by long hours spent chipping away the white, sappy rind to get at the scarlet dye-crystals that gave the wood its main value in Europe.

The men's hands and arms were stained red, their clothes impregnated with the strong, sweet smell of the yellow logwood flowers. On Saturdays they left their saws and axes and went hunting. When they killed a steer they quartered the corpse, threw away the bones, and cut a big hole in each section. Each of the four hunters thrust his head through a hole, 'put the flesh on like a frock', and trudged back to camp, which was sited as near the shore as possible 'for the benefit of the sea-breezes'. There the meat was boucanned or 'jerked' (dried crisp in the sun).

Trading ketches were expected to give free drinks on arrival. Dampier noted that if a captain was niggardly with the rum, they would 'pay him with their worst wood' – a load of hollow logs filled with dirt. But if he proved to be 'one of the old buccaneers, a hearty brave toss-pot, a trump, a true twopenny', the cutters would spend prodigally, 'carousing and firing off guns three or four days together'.

When he came to write up his journals, Dampier looked back in censure. The companies of Terminus Lagoon were, he now affected to believe, a deplorable, feckless lot set on 'the squandering of life away'. Any man who came there with sober habits was soon debauched by 'the Old Standards'. Some reprobates who found the work too hard preferred to spend their time sacking Indian villages, keeping the women 'for their solace' and selling the males as slaves. But their own lives were chancy. Fever, the guinea-worm (which bored deep into the leg and caused festering sores), hurricanes and torrential rains were ever-present threats. Spanish raiders burned the camps from time to time and carried the loggers off to slavery in the silver-mines. Captain Buckenham, once notorious as the heartiest toss-pot among the Old Standards, ended his days as a slave in Mexico City, 'with a log chained to his legs and a basket at his back, crying "Bread" along the streets for a Baker his master'. Like others who tried the alternative of the logwood trade, Dampier, who was plagued by guinea-worms and blown out of his 'estate' by a 'South' (hurricane), found pirating preferable to the rigours of One Bush Key.

Père Labat, a Jesuit priest who arrived in the West Indies in 1694 during the last years of the flibustier binge, found the buccaneers no worse, and sometimes better, than most French officials and planters. 'One would see nothing but mulattoes in our islands', he wrote, 'were it not that the King has imposed a fine of 2,000 lbs of sugar if a man is convicted of fathering one. . . . But in seeking to remedy the scandal the door has been opened to the crime of abortion, procured by female slaves with the help of their masters.' Over-inquisitive priests were apt to find themselves accused of being the lecherous culprits, and literally laughed out of court. Labat contrasts such unedifying behaviour with the ostentatious piety of some buccaneers who put in to Martinique with two English prizes and immediately presented themselves for confession: 'The Mass of the Virgin was celebrated with all solemnity and I blessed three large loaves given by the Captain and his officers, who arrived at the church accompanied by drummers and trumpeters. At the beginning of Mass their corvette fired a salute with all her guns. At the Elevation she fired another salvo, at the Benediction a third, and finally a fourth when we sang the Te Deum. All the filibusters contributed 30 sols to the sacristy. . . . They generally give a portion of their prizes to the churches, especially if church ornaments or linen happen to be among the items captured.'

Sometimes, however, an unrepentant Old Standard marred the Runyonesque atmosphere of hearts-of-gold contrition, as when 'one of the pirates played the fool during the Elevation, and being rebuked by the captain, replied insolently with a horrible oath. Captain Daniel promptly drew his pistol, shot him, and swore by God that he would do the same to anyone else who showed disrespect to the Holy Sacrifice.' When the Mass (celebrated on board ship) was over, the corpse was thrown into the sea and Daniel paid the priest with 'some valuable presents', including a Negro slave boy – who turned out to have been stolen from M. Vambel, a Martinique planter. Labat, who arranged for M. Vambel to be paid for the boy, took a generous commission as go-between in this and other matters of the kind, and clearly enjoyed his diplomatic role in buccaneer communities where no one had clean hands, even though they liked to pretend they had.

'Roving, the sack of Cartagena, and the loot from the Jamaican raids has filled Saint-Domingue with gold and silver,' he noted in 1698. 'When I was at Léogane I saw many chaises and carosses and only the very poorest settlers rode on horseback. They all gamble to excess and vie with each other in flaunting their wealth. Everyone likes to forget what he was when he came to the island, and I could name quite a few who came out as *engagés* and were sold to the buccaneers, but who are now such great seigneurs that they cannot walk a step but must always ride in their carriage drawn by six horses, complete with Negro coachman and postilions.'

This was the kind of apotheosis achieved by Morgan and some of his cronies in Jamaica, by Condent and his men in Mauritius, and, it may be, by John Taylor and his gang in Portobello or Cuba after their return from the Indian Ocean. This, not Libertalia, had been the ambition of most, if not all, pirates who had a mind to settle anywhere. The Caribbean, that Mecca and nursery of pirates, had not changed much in the two centuries since Columbus had bewailed the laziness of the first Spanish emigrants ('those who came out as miners, labourers and scullions will not stir from their homes unless they are carried on palanquins').

The pirate, like the colonial, dream was one of infinite idleness made possible by slave labour and typified by the Surinam planter on his way to church, followed by a native servant girl ready to light his cigar and carrying a cushion for him to kneel on. Charles Kingsley came pretty near the mark in one stanza of *The Last Buccaneer*:

Oh sweet it was in Avès to hear the landward breeze,
A-swing with good tobacco in a net between the trees,
With a negro lass to fan you while you listened to the roar
Of the breakers on the reef outside that never touched the shore.

Such ignoble ambitions have been shared by men on the run, or in a rut, for thousands of years. Pirates were no exception, and it has become fashionable to sneer at the very notion that some of them may have been drawn by something more than a passion for loot. Yet this kind of reductive platitude tells more about those who employ it than

'. . . that old breed of rovers whose port lay always a little further on' : one of Mervyn Peake's illustrations for Treasure Island.

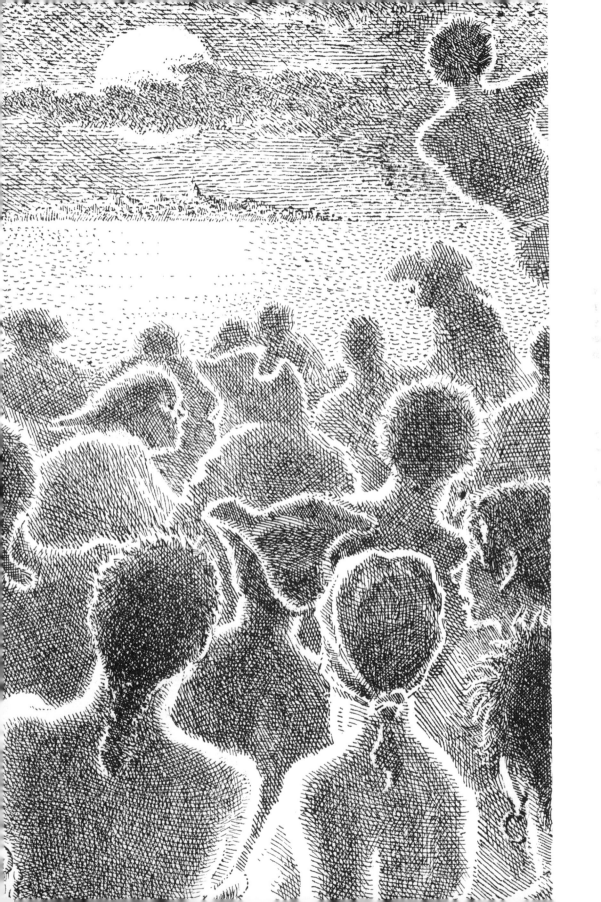

about those whom it is meant to cut down to size. Seventy years ago, in his book *On the Spanish Main*, John Masefield, who had spent half a long lifetime at sea, wrote: 'These men were of that old breed of rovers whose port lay always a little further on. If they lived riotously, let it be argued in their favour that at least they lived. . . . We think them terrible. Life itself is terrible. But it was not so terrible to them; for they were comrades, with the strength to live their own lives. They may laugh at those who condemn with the hate of impotence.'

Purple padding? Romantic rhetoric? Maybe, but people cannot live by bread, resignation, and adventure playgrounds alone. More than ever today, in the tightening nets of control (for their own good, of course), they search for precedents, clutch at straws, of freedom and audacity. However shiftily and fitfully, the pirates did fashion a kind of defiant life-style, and in the days before the grey hordes of honest labour coagulated to do battle with freebooting capitalism and pimping parsons, they offered a lovingly magnified gleam of guerilla truculence.

One could argue that the pirates' true heirs are the mobile terrorists – voluntary outsiders flourishing a variety of causes yet all flying the black jack of anti-reductive defiance. But perhaps their closest counterparts are, as they were, totally apolitical and willing to play the System with a commission of sorts. For instance the young professional hobo quoted in Kenneth Allsop's *Hard Travellin'*: 'I have an air bag and a brown suit and a pair of Pan-American wings I pin on. That gives a vague impression of being a serviceman and motorists come across with lifts. . . . I don't owe the bank 3,000 dollars for a car and I'm not killing myself to meet repayments on a house, so naturally I'm a failure. Beautiful!'

Pirates were not particularly sadistic or lustful, but it would be silly to deny that they enjoyed their bursts of mayhem and fornication. 'All right,' says Alex, the juvenile rip, in *A Clockwork Orange*, 'I do bad, what with crasting and tolchocks and carves with the britva and the old in-and-out . . . and you can't run a country with every chelloveck comporting himself in my manner of the night. Badness is of the self, the one, the you or me on our oddy knockies. . . . But the not-self cannot have the bad, meaning they of the government and the judges and the schools, because they cannot allow the self. And is not our modern history, my brothers, the story of brave malenky selves fighting these big machines? I am serious with you, brothers, over this. But what I do I do because I like to do.' The pirate legend commemorates and reflects a dream of irresponsibility, lethal larkiness, and, above all, mobility: a life as clear of obligations as the hulls of the pirates' lovingly-careened ships were of speed-reducing growths.

Bibliography

List of Illustrations

Index

Bibliography

I General

Andrews, K. H., *Elizabethan Privateering : English Privateering During the Spanish War, 1585–1603* (London and New York, 1964). Authoritative and enthralling.

Belgrave, Sir Charles, *The Pirate Coast* (London, 1966; New York, 1967).

Brøndsted, Johannes, *The Vikings* (Harmondsworth and Baltimore, 1973).

Burney, James, *The History of the Buccaneers of America* (London, 1949; New York, 1951). Reprinted from the edition of 1816. Wonderfully readable and judicious.

Cabal, Juan, *Piracy and Pirates* (London, 1957). Translated from the Spanish.

Chatterton, E. Keble, *The Romance of Piracy* (London, 1914; Philadelphia, 1915).

Cleugh, James, *Prince Rupert : A Biography* (London, 1934).

Course, Captain A. G., *Pirates of the Eastern Seas* (London, 1966; New York, 1968).

Defoe, Daniel (Captain Charles Johnson), *A General History of the Robberies and Murders of the Most Notorious Pirates, 1717–1724* (London and Columbia, S.C., 1972). Edited and with a long and useful introduction by Manuel Schonhorn.

Earle, Peter, *Corsairs of Malta and Barbary* (London and New York, 1970).

Ellms, Charles, *The Pirates' Own Book, or Authentic Narratives of the Lives, Exploits and Executions of the Most Celebrated Sea Robbers* (Philadelphia, 1837).

Exquemelin, Alexander, *The Buccaneers of America* (Harmondsworth and Baltimore, 1969). First published in English in 1684.

Fisher, Sir Godfrey, *Barbary Legend: War, Trade and Piracy in North Africa, 1415–1830* (Oxford and New York, 1957).

Forester, C. S., *The Barbary Pirates* (London, 1956; New York, 1970).

Fowles, John, *Shipwreck* (London, 1974).

Gosse, Philip, *The Pirates' Who's Who* (London and Boston, 1924). Mainly a useful précis, arranged in alphabetical order, of the chief characters and incidents in the histories of Exquemelin and Defoe; with an entertaining, if over-facetious, introduction.

—— *The History of Piracy* (London and New York, 1932).

Haring, C. H., *The Buccaneers in the West Indies in the Seventeenth Century* (London and New York, 1910). Brilliant and scholarly.

Hobsbawm, Eric, *Bandits* (London and New York, 1969). A social history based on a critical study of bandit legend, which has some parallels with pirate legend.

Innes, Brian, *The Book of Pirates* (London, 1966).

Kemp, P. H., and Christopher Lloyd, *The Brethren of the Coast : British and French Buccaneers in the South Seas* (London, 1960; New York, 1961).

Labat, Père, *Memoirs 1693–1705* (London, 1970). With an introduction by Philip Gosse.

Leslie, Robert C. (ed.), *The Journal of Captain Woodes Rogers 1708–11* (London, 1894).

Lloyd, Christopher, *Sir Francis Drake* (London, 1957; Mystic, Conn., 1966).

—— *William Dampier* (London, 1966; Hamden, Conn., 1967).

Lydon, James G., *Pirates, Privateers and Profits* (Boston, 1971).

Maclay, Edgar Stanton, *A History of American Privateers* (New York, 1899; London, 1900).

Masefield, John, *On the Spanish Main* (London and New York, 1925). First published in 1908, still sound and thrilling.

Ormerod, Henry, *Piracy in the Ancient World* (London, 1924).

Parry, J. H., and P. M. Sherlock, *A Short History of the West Indies* (London and New York, 1956). A very good coverage indeed.

Pringle, Patrick, *Jolly Roger: The Story of the Great Age of Piracy* (London and New York, 1953). A near-classic, not so wide-ranging as Gosse's *History*, but relying less on purely literary sources and much stronger on social history.

Roberts, W. Adolphe, *Sir Henry Morgan* (London and New York, 1933). Straining a bit after local colour, but well researched, intelligent and exciting.

Russell of Liverpool, Lord, *The French Corsairs* (London, 1970).

Rutter, Owen, *The Pirate Wind: Tales of the Sea Robbers of Malaya* (London, 1930).

Severin, Timothy, *The Golden Antilles* (London and New York, 1970). Lively chapters on Raleigh and the buccaneers, and good on the acquisitive society in the Caribbean.

Stark, Francis R., *The Abolition of Privateering and the Declaration of Paris* (New York, 1897). A short, scholarly, incisive thesis which packs in a lot of information and historical background.

Tenenti, Alberto, *Piracy and the Decline of Venice* (London and Berkeley, 1967).

Williams, Eric, *From Columbus to Castro: The History of the Caribbean 1492–1969* (London, 1970; New York, 1971).

Williams, Neville, *Captains Outrageous: Seven Centuries of Piracy* (London, 1961; New York, 1962). Supplements the histories of Gosse and Pringle with much new material from official records and other contemporary documents. Probably the most authoritative survey of the subject from a British point of view.

Winston, Alexander, *No Purchase, No Pay: Morgan, Kidd and Woodes Rogers in the Great Age of Privateers and Pirates 1665–1715* (London, 1970). Originally published as *No Man Knows My Grave* (Boston, 1969).

Woodbury, George, *The Great Days of Piracy* (New York, 1951; London, 1954).

Wycherley, George, *Buccaneers of the Pacific* (Indianapolis, 1928; London, 1929).

Anyone really interested in the subject should consult the comprehensive and fully annotated catalogue on Piracy and Privateering in the Library of the National Maritime Museum, Greenwich.

II Pirate Ballads

John Masefield's anthology, *A Sailor's Garland* (London, 1908; New York, 1924), has a very useful selection. F. J. Child (ed.), *The English and Scottish Popular Ballads* (New York, 1965, 4 vols.) has many versions of 'Sir Andrew Barton', 'The High Coasts of Barbary' and 'Captain Ward and the Rainbow', with historical background notes; so does B. H. Bronson, *Traditional Tunes of the Child Ballads* (Princeton, 1959–72, 4 vols.). W. M. Doerflinger, *Shantymen and Shantyboys: Songs of the Sailor and the Lumberman* (New York, 1951) contains sets of 'The Flying Cloud', 'Bold Manning' and 'The

Bold Princess Royal'. W. R. Mackenzie, *Ballads and Sea Songs from Nova Scotia* (Cambridge, Mass., 1928) has the John Paul Jones ballad and an item called 'Kelly the Pirate'.

The two ballads on Captain Avery/Every and his men can be found in C. H. Firth, *Naval Songs and Ballads* (Navy Records Society, London, 1908). I am deeply grateful to A. L. Lloyd for supplying me with copies of them, and with an invaluable bibliographical guide to the subject. In his introduction to John Ashton, *Real Sailor Songs* (first published 1891, reissued 1973 by Broadsheet King, 15 Mortimer Terrace, London N.W.5), A. L. Lloyd not only gives some graphic details about conditions in the navy and merchant marine in the eighteenth and nineteenth centuries, but quotes a number of rare ballads.

All the above volumes (with the exception of Firth's *Naval Songs and Ballads*), and many others, can be consulted in the Vaughan Williams Memorial Library at Cecil Sharp House, headquarters of the English Folk Dance and Song Society.

The 'Dialogue between the Ghost of Captain Kidd and the Napper in the Strand' is in the British Museum (C.121.g.9.134).

List of Illustrations

NMM: National Maritime Museum, Greenwich

Colour illustrations

Black-and-white illustrations

Index